D0780883

High Performing Teams

. . . in brief

High Performing Teams

Teams

. . . in brief

Michael Colenso

Butterworth-Heinemann
Linacre House, Jordan Hill, Oxford OX2 8DP
A division of Reed Educational and Professional Publishing Ltd

℞ A member of the Reed Elsevier plc group

OXFORD   BOSTON   JOHANNESBURG
MELBOURNE   NEW DELHI   SINGAPORE

First published 1997

© Michael Colenso 1997

All rights reserved. No part of this publication may be reproduced in any
material form (including photocopying or storing in any medium by
electronic means and whether or not transiently or incidentally to some
other use of this publication) without the written permission of the
copyright holder except in accordance with the provisions of the
Copyright, Designs and Patents Act 1988 or under the terms of a licence
issued by the Copyright Licensing Agency Ltd, 90 Tottenham Court Road,
London, England W1P 9HE. Applications for the copyright holder's
written permission to reproduce any part of this publication should be
addressed to the publisher

British Library Cataloguing in Publication Data
A catalogue record for this book is available from the British Library

ISBN 0 7506 3354 9

658.4036
C69h

Composition by Scribe Design, Gillingham, Kent
Printed and bound in Great Britain by
Biddles Ltd, Guildford and King's Lynn

Contents

University Libraries
Carnegie Mellon University
Pittsburgh PA 15213-3890

Preface

The literature on teaming is not sparse. As I reviewed the books that were around, it seemed to me that every other year a really good one was published. High Performing Teams conforms to this alternate year pattern.

On the other hand the journal literature on teams simply floods out all the time. This indicates how much interest, experimentation, research and solid effort is being invested in implementing the concepts of teams and empowerment. It seems that the whole world is at it, and rightly so!

Butterworth-Heinemann/Institute of Management's In brief ... series is an excellent idea. With them, I believe that we are less in need of information than we are of advice. The In brief ... series acknowledges this. In writing this book, I have been speaking personally and directly to an overworked line manager, perhaps even one doing a formal course while trying to keep the lid on events at work at the same time.

I have tried to treat you, the reader, with respect and sympathy. Mindful as I am of your time pressures, I may not always have balanced the argument nicely. I am unrepentant in acknowledging bias. In fact I hope this will help you more, because the bias stems from long experience as a line manager, trainer and consultant. I hope you will find my blend of bias and balance right for you.

In writing the book, a number of people have helped enormously:

- My daughter, Jane, has bombarded me with literature, material, contacts and advice. She has consistently broadened the purview of the book.
- My son, Peter, proofed the manuscript for me, wrestled my often contorted prose to the ground, and imposed a measure of consistency on punctuation and grammar.
- Anita Cumberpatch at the Institute of Management has been the conduit of delivery of IM's superb information services. A service so good one wants to keep it a secret but, in honesty, cannot.

Preface

- The people at Butterworth-Heinemann, Jacqui Shanahan and Diane Scarlett, who actually return telephone calls, lifted my spirits when I was blue and chided me only gently at missed deadlines.
- Maxine Clark and Sue Giles at the Benefits Agency who provided, in their case report, one of the best examples of empowerment and leaderless teaming I have encountered.
- Above all, Joan, my wife, who knew when to tell me to stop snipping dead heads off the fuschias and to get back to work; who appeared at critical moments with a restorative glass of wine; and who regularly carted me off on 'outings' when she judged I had communed with the cathode rays long enough.

Michael Colenso
Claygate
Autumn 1996

Acknowledgements

The Team Empowerment model which appears on page 43 is taken from Wellins, Byham and Wilson Empowered Teams: Creating self directed work groups that improve quality, productivity and participation. The table is reproduced with permission of the publishers Jossey Bass Inc., in San Francisco.

Belbin's 'Nine Team Roles', which appear on page 84, are reproduced from his book Team Roles at Work, 1993, with permission of the publishers, Butterworth–Heinemann.

The quotation about teams being inherently inferior to individuals which appears on page 78 is taken from Robbins, and Finley Why Teams Don't Work: What went wrong and how to make it right, published by Peterson's/Pacesetter Books, Princeton New Jersey. It is reproduced with permission of Harvey Robbins. Mr Robbins has also consented to his e-mail address being included in this book under the Direct Access section on page 165.

The person specification for successful business process re-engineering which appears on page 117 is taken from Hammer The Reengineering Revolution Handbook published by Harper Collins in 1996. The quotation is reproduced with permission of the author, Michael Hammer.

The Leader/Manager model on page 132 appears with permission of Wilson Learning Corporation, Eden Prairie, Minnesota. It appears in Wilson's programme The Leader Manager.

The quotation on team learning which appears on page 145 is taken from Senge The Fifth Discipline: The art and practice of the learning organization, 1990. It is reproduced with permission of Random House UK Ltd. and of Bantam, Doubleday, Dell Publishing Group in New York.

What is in this book – a user's guide

Introduction

This book is part of a series which seeks to provide briefing for executives about the major management theories and processes which go to make up the contents of the tool kit of the contemporary manager. It is written for managers who are involved in thinking about strategy, or involved in implementing change. It is meant to provide concise and relevant help but at the same time to reflect the debate which inevitably surrounds each subject. The editors advise that authors should envisage a reader with five minutes to spare in order to get their heads around a subject.

Management books are rarely read cover to cover. Usually readers approach them in one of two ways:

- from the front, scanning a list of contents to gain direct access to the subject of interest;
- from the back, using the index for the same purpose.

To help the people who favour the frontal approach, the map which follows is an expanded list of contents and it should inform you better where to dive in. Also at the start of each chapter is a brief summary of what it talks about. The index, at the back, is a standard one but properly done.

That is about the best one can do without recourse to random access.

A consequence of trying to design a book to match the way readers will probably use it is that the writer has to convey a good overview in a relatively small number of words, making the assumption that other parts of the book, where the subject may appear in some other guise, have not been read. Cross-referring is one way of handling the problem; here the risk is that the reader runs out of fingers to keep his/her place in different sections. The other solution is to give a brief restatement of the argument in its other guise. The risk here is that you get repetitive. I have done both in this book, and I hope to have got the balance right.

Remembering the editors' descriptor of the five-minute window of the reader/manager, you will find at the end of almost all sections an executive summary. This enables you to extract the meat from the section which has preceded it.

An e-mail address on which you can reach me is in the back of the book and I would appreciate your feedback.

Map of the book

	Sections and content	Page

What is in this book – a user's guide

What is in this book – a user's guide

Chapter	Sections and content	Page
14. Where to Find Out More Gives a very biased account of the best sources of more information. Keeps the advice short.	Suggests: • The best books on the subject • Journals and literature search facilities • The best international training companies and some specialists	160
Bibliography and reference	A list of the books and journal articles which have been mentioned in the text or which have made important contributions to the author's thinking	166

2

What high performing teams are all about

This chapter sets out to establish a common understanding of what teams are and why they are used in organizations. It gives a broad view of the experience of organizations in using teams. The executive summary provides a useful reminder outlining preconditions for success.

What is a team?

The slaves of the Egyptians hauling forty-ton blocks of limestone up the side of the great pyramid of Khufu were a team of a sort in 2600 BC. Four thousand six hundred years later, many employees would argue that the same Egyptian managerial principles survive as we move into the second millennium AD. Whether true or not, those principles provide a means of getting things done through the deployment of a number of people of varied functional capability in pursuit of a shared objective.

Almost everyone has some sort of experience of teams and teaming. Almost everyone has, at some time or another, been a member of a team. Millions of people are still members of teams, and millions more are vicariously involved, often passionately, in the fortunes of teams they support. Teams and teaming have an emotional content conveying feelings of mutual support, camaraderie, warmth, inclusion, success and belonging. Indeed the word 'team' probably comes from Old English and meant 'family' or 'line of descendants'.

Teams are also associated with providing additional strength or power. We speak of a team of oxen pulling a plough, or horses drawing a stagecoach. Yoking in more people or animals to provide the motive power or ability to fulfil a project predates even our Egyptian team. Nowadays we call it synergy: the whole being greater than the sum of the individual parts.

Three strands constantly intertwine in teams and teaming:

- commonality of objective or purpose;
- belonging and being a part of something successful;
- synergy – achieving more collectively than can be achieved by individuals acting outside a team environment.

These strands apply as consistently in the contemporary business context as they do in pyramid building, sport, plough pulling or whatever. Plainly, in the right circumstances, teaming can provide significant benefits and it is this that has attracted organizations.

Why organizations are using teams

The primary and overwhelming organizational motive behind the use of teams is performance enhancement. Unlocking the synergy leads to enhanced or improved levels of performance, however that may be defined. In the tough competitive climate in which organizations now operate, performance enhancement can mean containing cost, improving product/service quality, getting to the market faster, improving customer satisfaction, being able to enact radical change quickly. For many organizations these are strategic imperatives of the highest importance. Even if these attributes are not issues of survival for an organization, they are, at least, components of organizational fitness, the attainment of which must be taken seriously.

Organizations obviously respond to their environments in a number of ways; one of the most prevalent actions they have taken during the 1980s and 1990s has been the reduction in the size of their workforces. People have been stripped out at all levels, middle management paying a particularly high price. Reducing the number of people employed has a consequence beyond saving in costs; it also means that surviving employees have to work more closely together and to be more flexible in order to provide continuity of operations and services. Many companies have sought, by the development of teams, to achieve this.

The quality movement, now less of a movement than a licence to play in the game, has also used the synergy of teaming to promote the improvement of goods and services to both internal and external customers. Cross-functional teams have been particularly effective in both attaining and sustaining quality improvement.

Manufacturing cell technology has also promoted teaming use. This implies redesigning the flow of Henry Ford's traditional production line and aggregating mixtures of processes within a manufacturing sequence. At its apex we have the now famous Volvo experiment of a team being responsible for making the whole car. But cell technology is also used to manufacture sub-assemblies linking together the various skills and capabilities of a group and unlocking their synergy through teaming.

With the more recent rise of process re-engineering, many organizations are moving towards process technology: the redesign of work around a group of related tasks which together add value for the customer. Typically these related tasks are previously diffused throughout the organization, embedded in a number of functional departments.

Taking an order and shipping it to a customer might successively involve Sales Department activity, an invoicing activity, credit checking in Finance, inventory updates in Operations, picking and packing in a warehouse and so on. Locating these processes within a single unit of responsibility is enhanced by turning that unit into a cross-functional team.

Behind all these applications is the attempt to improve performance through teaming, usually after an initial redesign, re-equipping or reorganization. Sometimes it has worked, sometimes it has not.

How successful?

When organizations are polled as to their experiences of going a teaming route, a number of positive answers emerge. Those which have achieved successful applications report an improvement in the way the company has been able to unlock the skills and experience of team members. This has usually produced an improvement in the way resources have been used with consequent increases in efficiency, effectiveness or productivity.

An improvement in communications across the organization is usually reported, and so is the visible degree of co-operation between departments, functions or teams. The feeling among staff members of increased personal ownership, responsibility and buy-in are usually deemed to have improved as well.

Discernible, however, is a suggestion that the potential of the teams has yet to be fully realized. The feeling is usually that there is more to be achieved, more to be gained. A lurking sense of marginal disappointment is often evident even in successful applications. Sometimes this is phrased in terms of the best being yet to come.

The difficulties reported as a result of moving to teaming centre overwhelmingly on the time it takes to get teams up and running. Even well-prepared organizations are surprised that it takes so long. There is also consensus that the change in the role of managers to which teams report (as distinct from team leaders) is radical and unexpectedly difficult. Manager-as-facilitator and manager-as-coach roles, even when anticipated and sometimes even trained for, often turn out to be deeply unsatisfactory to line managers.

Organizational structure sometimes gets in the way of teams, with friction developing around turf issues. For example, the team believes that to be effective certain categories of decision should be vested in it, while people or departments which are currently responsible for those decisions may not be ready to abdicate them. Organizational culture is often antithetical to teams too; successful teams can be perceived as threats within the organization at large. This can escalate into corporate slugging matches and the worst manifestations of internal politics.

The lessons

As we get deeper into this book the experience of others will start to show that there are considerable investments to be made – investments of planning, managerial time, training and opportunity cost in creating high performing teams. In fact the manager is ill-advised to embark on a team building route unless:

■ there is clarity about what it is expected will be achieved by organizing and operating as a team or teams;
■ there is certainty that teaming is the best or only way to achieve the strategy or objectives;
■ the organization is absolutely committed to succeeding, which will imply un-learning and re-learning for everyone involved.

There is a very punishing downside to starting out on a team-building process and failing. Employees and colleagues generally welcome the initiative and embark on it with enthusiasm. When the process starts to hit trouble, and it will, managers have to resist the temptation to fall into the Egyptian-pyramid-building school of teaming and hold out for something closer to the model of the high performing team.

If the manager and the team are unsuccessful in unlocking the collective magic of synergy, the initiative will fail with two probable consequences:

■ Objectives will not have been achieved.
■ People will become cynical of the process and managers will not be given a second chance until they can overcome that cynicism.

Many organizations are littered with 'teams' which are not high performing at all and will probably never be so. Often it suits members to participate in meetings, misleadingly designated 'team meetings', simply to trade information, use the forum to laud their own activities and complain about the non-compliance of others.

If, on the other hand, the manager succeeds in developing a high performing team, the pay-offs will be significant and the work unit will have some invaluable capabilities:

14

- improved productivity because energy is focused, purpose is shared, objectives are clear and outcomes agreed;
- fast response and increased flexibility to change and adapt, also interchangeability of function among team members;
- enhanced problem solving – innovation and creativity;
- high communication within the team and outside it.

Members of high performing teams have an enhanced sense of self-worth and an appropriate sense of the value that they individually and as a team add to the organization. They start to become self-managing because of the sense of shared responsibility that the team develops. They are also self-critical in the most creative sense.

The view is mixed

There are a number of books, courses, development programmes etc. which can help the line manager start the processes of creating a high performing team. More recently we have seen a stream of publications about why teams have not worked. In fact the Financial Times 1996 Best Management Book (Americas Section) is the highly recommendable Why Teams Don't Work. What Went Wrong and How to Make it Right by Harvey Robbins and Michael Finley (2.1). This is, at the time of writing, just the most recent of a number of titles, journal articles and studies which look at the reasons high performance has not been achieved in teams. Even the prestigious Harvard Business Review published a case study in November 1994 entitled The Team That Wasn't (2.2). In it Susan Wetlaufer, a former Bain employee, lays out the case and invites the diagnoses and advice of a number of luminaries in the field.

It seems unfortunate that the bias of recent publications is towards investigating reasons for failing to produce high performing teams. I believe it is also a strong message that organizations often find it a lot harder to achieve than they ever imagined. The point behind all this is that, just as the Liturgy advises that marriage is not to be lightly or thoughtlessly undertaken, so should it be with trying to create high performing teams.

On the other hand, the modern business environment, for reasons we will get to later in this book, will increasingly

High Performing Teams

require the qualities of high performing teams as organizational and operational capabilities. Essentially the successful team environment produces performance enhancement for individuals within it and for the organization at large. Teaming often provides an organizational effectiveness which usually exceeds that achieved by traditional hierarchical chains of command. It also provides the additional flexibility to sustain and absorb change. The disciplines and processes of high performing teams provide empowerment and purpose for employees and usually greatly improve job satisfaction.

There is evidence that the move, which has been apparent for a number of years, towards more people-centred companies is gaining momentum. Under the chairmanship of Sir Anthony Cleaver, The Royal Society for the encouragement of Arts, Manufactures and Commerce recently conducted an extended inquiry into the nature of the company of the future. Their results were published in Tomorrow's Company: The Role of Business in a Changing World, 1995 (2.3).

Evidence is adduced in the report to support the view that superior company performance is achieved in those company environments in which employees have the benefit of formal systems for their appraisal, the analysis of their training needs, the delivery of training, and assessment of the results achieved (Britain's Investors in People standard).

More importantly, more company directors (67 per cent) now see greater value in team work and long-term, trust-based relationships than those who value adversarial, power-based relationships.

Hard evidence of results suggests, and an increasingly convinced majority of managers believe, that teaming provides a viable managerial system. Line managers who have achieved this will ruefully acknowledge that it was fine when you got there, but the journey was longer and more difficult than anticipated. Above all, an organizational transition to teaming changes the way almost everything is done and the jobs and responsibilities of all the employees. Small wonder that organizations often put a toe in the water first by running pilot teams and learning from them.

What I hope to achieve in this book is a balanced account of the subject which should at least equip the reader to judge when to try it and to provide some help in how (s)he might successfully achieve high performing teams.

Executive summary

Preconditions	**Failure**	**Success**
for high performance	*(looks like . . .)*	*high performance (looks like . . .)*
Clarity of outcome and criteria for success	No consensus, people pulling in different directions	Team has clear focus on agreed criteria + consensus on priorities
Commitment to unlocking team synergy	Disbelief and cynicism – 'flavour of the day' accusations	Preparedness to be open, frank, self-critical and mutually supportive
High levels of effective communication	Communication takes place in the corridor or behind closed doors	Members talk freely at team meetings – do not feel intimidated or threatened
Preparedness to take some risks . . .	Risk averse – 'don't rock the boat'	Team evaluates risk and takes considered decisions
and . . .	and . . .	and . . .
search for innovative solutions	'it will never fly'	actively searches for different and imaginative approaches
Preparedness to accept a shared responsibility for the team, its successes and its failures	Refusal to participate in shared responsibility: 'it's up to you', 'it's not my job'	Committed to succeeding and confident enough to take responsibility for the team's decisions

3

How the high performing team concept developed

This chapter provides the historical context which has helped teaming become a tool used in the management of organizations. It traces the development of teaming from early research through early applications and the Japanese influence, and indicates contributions made by more recent work on team development.

Background

It is a mistake to think that any group of people acting together constitute a team. Quite often managers will refer to their 'team' when in reality they are dealing with a group of individuals whose commonality of purpose is simply to prevent themselves from being overwhelmed by the workload. A team in the process of formation will at least be aspiring to the characteristics of the ☺ – SUCCESS column at the end of Chapter 2. A high performing team will have most of these characteristics in place, and it will be observing and monitoring its performance against them.

We know that the slaves of the Egyptians were not willing participants in the particular variety of team management prevalent at the time. Indeed the children of Israel departed for the dubious pleasures of crossing the Sinai peninsula and risking the parting of the Red Sea rather than continuing to participate.

How the high performing team concept developed

The early Olympiads developed simple team sports in relay races and these had three high performing team characteristics:

- Clarity of required outcome;
- willing, probably enthusiastic participation;
- exercising maximum individual effort in support of the team as a whole.

Military applications of teaming abound from the earliest times that bands of people either attacked their foes or defended their loved ones. Certainly armies, navies and airforces develop and deploy a great variety of specialist skills that are characterized by interdependence, mutual support, and the achievement of synergy. The armed forces are also, when they are needed, pretty clear about what success looks like.

Perhaps the great difference between the military and business environment of teams is the ingredient that encourages the team to manage itself. The armed forces necessarily work on a far less flexible chain of command than does the average business and, furthermore, the latitude for collective decision making is, unsurprisingly, severely constrained and highly situational.

Interestingly, the thinking and research which have driven the business applications of team development rely hardly at all on the military tradition, and little on the wealth of experience in sport, though they do use military and sporting vocabulary and they draw on both areas for analogies. They are unable to implement most military and sporting models, however, because a fundamentally different relationship exists between employer and employee than exists between officer and enlisted person or coach and player.

The social psychologists

Team development in business has drawn more on social psychology for its raw material and initially on research into the dynamics of groups working together. A quick cherry-picking review of some of the thinking and research the social psychologists have provided probably helps a contemporary manager in thinking about developing high performing teams. Based presumably on the principle that if you could bottle it you could sell it, there has been considerable research into what goes on in high performing teams to release or generate the synergy by which their performance is achieved.

In the USA in the late 1940s, a number of researchers observed the behaviour of problem solving teams and developed some valuable work on group roles. Benne and Sheets in the late 1940s probably pioneered this activity but others, like the highly successful social psychologists Kretch and Crutchfield, and later C. J. Margerison in the 1970s, also developed well-observed and useful analyses of the processes which occurred in a business-based team environment.

Most of this work uses the word 'roles' to describe processes and the word rather clouds the clarity of the research. 'Roles' implies natural or required behaviour on the part of the participants. What I believe these researchers actually contributed was a series of useful analyses of what needs to go on in a group in order to solve problems.

The 'roles', or more accurately team activities, fall into some clear categories:

- those associated with initiating events, re-aligning or steering the team to keep it on course;
- those that request and provide information and opinion;
- those associated with 'housekeeping' – calling and recording meetings etc.;
- those associated with the **process** which is at the heart of the team's activity.

It is here, in what I have called the process area, that the value of this early work contributes most to understanding the development of high performing teams.

A team must be jollied along to get on with things; it must keep its spirits and hence its energy high. The best high performing teams have quite a bit of fun too – and this is both a reason for and a consequence of high performance. Researchers variously called this the Energizer role (Benne and Sheets) or the Thruster role (Margerison).

Belbin's (see below) Shapers and Plants also contributed somewhat to this function.

How the high performing team concept developed

Every team goes through the process of testing the utility of the ideas it generates. This involves imagining examples of implementing ideas; considering consequences and looking at the contingent or reactive behaviour and events that implementation might generate. Essentially this is a verbal and imaginative testing procedure. It is where most of this discussion of the team is centred. Researchers called it variously an Elaborator role, Explorer role, Monitor-evaluator etc.

Teams need to look at the interconnectedness of ideas and information. They need to recognize when the team has reached consensus or even an interim conclusion so that decisions or views are consolidated and rolled forward. Often, but not necessarily, this is the chair's activity. Arbitrator, Controller, Completer/Finisher are role descriptors early researchers used.

There is also a need for the team to control its quality; it must test its overall performance and progress against the standards it has set for itself, the progress it is making against its objectives, and in high performing teams, what the team is learning. Role descriptors like Upholder, Orienter, Teamworker etc. have been applied here.

Belbin

Influential work in the UK was done by R. M. Belbin (3.1, 3.2) working at the Henley Management College. Over a number of years Belbin observed work groups or classes in progress at the Management College and defined a list of roles which are in some ways similar to the earlier work but tend to add more to the understanding of team processes. What distinguished Belbin's work was that it attempted to establish the relationship of these roles to the general success of the team. The hope was that a predictive model could be developed, and that has in part been achieved.

The usefulness of Belbin's Team Roles is enhanced because they have become the basis of objective assessment tests which are capable of predicting the likely behaviour of an individual in a team environment. Plainly this has value in building management teams. The extent of that value is, however, constrained by the availability of potential team members with typologies appropriate to filling all the designated roles. In general the process of determining who should be a member of a team would place more pressing criteria ahead of potential Team Role.

Belbin's Team Roles also provide an excellent basis for a team to discuss how it is operating. The context provided by objectively determined information on the roles present in the team allows members to evaluate the effectiveness of their processes. This is a subject to which we will return because there is evidence that one of the characteristics of high performing teams is that they pay a great deal of attention to assessing the way in which they are operating as well as to achieving results.

Team development

B. W. Tuckman, another psychologist, gave us in the 1970s an insight both useful and memorable to understanding the processes of team building. This is the team development model.

Forming   As the team comes together, tasks, rules and methods are established

Storming   Conflict starts to emerge as people test the task, each other and the leader

Norming   Co-operation starts to develop with some cohesion and unity of purpose; agreed cannons of behaviour emerge

Performing   Constructive work surges ahead; energy is focused

This model, and the numerous variants of it, provide one of the most useful tools for the leader who is trying to develop the team, and for the team itself to understand the behavioural patterns which its members are undergoing. We return to this model later in the book when we deal with developing high performance teams.

Encounter groups

Parallel to and contemporaneously with work on team roles or types, another strand has contributed, with varying degrees of success, to the development of teams in a business environment. This was the T-group movement or encounter groups developed by Carl Rogers. The word T-group has largely vanished from the contemporary management vocabulary but team-building exercises still rely heavily on the processes of encounter groups. Essentially these entail:

- making participants (team members) more sensitive to their own styles of behaviour and the effect this may have on others;
- helping them become more aware of the styles of others;
- requiring participants to suspend the learned judgements of a lifetime and to acknowledge that personal perceptions of rightway/wrongway might more sensibly be replaced by entertaining the possibility of 'different-way';
- creating analogies of real life in which participants live through situations or act out scenarios which illuminate their behaviour and the behaviour of others, and thus enable lessons to be learned.

Sir John Harvey-Jones briefly but vividly describes in his jovial and eminently readable book Making it Happen (3.3) his participation in a T-group in California in the late 1960s. A deeply frustrating day, in which two groups were required to reach agreement on a truly trivial subject, led him to frame some insights on mergers and take-overs which plainly stood him in good stead through a long and successful career at ICI.

The great outdoors

One of the modern manifestations of the encounter group is the outdoor or adventure practice of team development. Conforming to the encounter group criteria described above, the idea here is that the team collectively experiences a series of tasks which each is unlikely to have experienced individually before, and almost certainly never collectively as a team.

There are a number of well-known exercises like everybody scaling a fifteen-foot wall, or 'trust walks' where each member is charged with leading a blindfolded team colleague through an obstacle course. Problem solving exercises are set where seemingly inadequate resources are supplied to resolve logistical or spatial problems. Some exercises call for the demonstration of sheer bravery, especially the ropes courses, which are a great favourite in the USA, and many draw on the mental processes involved in martial arts such as karate.

There are literally hundreds of organizations which provide this sort of team development, and their continued success persists, in my experience, for two reasons. First this kind of activity is quite fun, and second the analogies provided enable participants to learn more about themselves. Team members also learn more about each other and they may develop more mutual trust and confidence in each other. There is little evidence to suggest that teams that have undergone this sort of development actually perform better than those that have not.

Early applications

In the UK in the 1940s a system called Socio-technical Design was developed at the Tavistock Institute in London. The system arose from work done in the coal-mining industry. Miners were formed into multi-skilled work groups to support a redesign of the way in which work was carried out underground. Teams were made responsible for their own decisions and for the flow of their work. The system achieved greater productivity and better morale within the workforce.

In the USA, Procter and Gamble based an entire new facility on the concept of self-managed teams. The success was so spectacular that Procter and Gamble treated it with the greatest confidentiality, classifying information about their team organization and treating it as a trade secret. Later Volvo, with the commissioning of its now famous Kalmar plant, broke new ground. Teams built complete components of cars as manufacturing cells rather than as operators supporting zones of a linear production line. This produced a dramatic increase in productivity and demonstrated the power of teaming.

The Japanese

While in the West there was considerable research into teaming, applications, such as those above, were limited. What changed the game and brought teaming up the management agenda was the increasingly convincing success that was being achieved by Japanese business.

By the late 1960s the post-war reconstruction of the Japanese economy was starting to be taken seriously in the West. The Japanese were using new forms of management which were in part the product of a formalized social system, but were also influenced by the need to compensate for a lack of raw materials, lack of industrial infrastructure and, in the early days of the reconstruction, lack of world-class competitive industrial skills.

The essential difference of the Japanese management system was that it asked more of its employees. Employees were asked to work harder, to become skilled at more than one job or activity, to take responsibility for the quality of what was being made, to contribute to the development and enhancement of the day-to-day processes they used. In other words, Japanese organizations were not only getting harder work from their employees, they were also accessing levels of positive involvement which were beyond mere productivity improvement.

More to the point, the products of this system were starting to undermine the market domination of the Western giants. Originally dismissed as cheap clones of superior Western technology, Japanese designed and manufactured goods were increasingly capturing the imagination and the spending power of the Western consumer. Nowhere was this more tellingly felt than at the heart of Western industrial might – the US motor car industry. It seemed hardly credible that GM, then the largest, most powerful, most profitable company in the history of time, should be losing market share to foreign imports in its prime product ranges and its domestic markets.

It was probably due to J. Edwards Deming, the American quality guru, that some of the secret ingredients of the Japanese management system started to flow westwards. Deming played an important role in the reconstruction of the Japanese economy but he also became the West's authority on how the Japanese did things. Quality circles were a very transferable construct, and quality circles rest on developing teams dedicated to improvement.

Teaming, it became clear, was a way by which some of the successful aspects of the Japanese management system could be transplanted into the radically different social environment of US and European business. It was the means by which the collective contribution of the workforce could be unlocked in the pursuit of improvement and efficiency.

The training companies

In the mid-1980s a number of international training companies put together team-building programmes which, because of their ingenuity and eclecticism, made, and are still making, important contributions to team development. These programmes bring together training and development models from a number of sources like interpersonal behaviour, communication, leadership etc. and then focus this material on workshops which are designed to accelerate the team development process.

There are almost countless training and development organizations offering team development programmes. Wilson Learning, Zenger Miller and Development Dimensions International (DDI) are organizations whose activities are worldwide and hence accessible to most readers of this book. (Contact addresses are included in chapter 14 'Where to Find Out More'.)

Wilson Learning provides, in three- or four-day facilitated sessions, a framework for teams to develop commonality of purpose and a vocabulary which will assist teams in analysing internal performance. This can be a valuable kick-start to a new team or a good therapy session for a 'stuck' team.

Zenger Miller too has good team development experience and has courses to offer which are well spoken of by users. Leading Teams: Mastering the New Role by Zenger, Musselwhite, Hurson and Perrin (3.4) looks like a useful book which, in conjunction with facilitated sessions, supports team development.

DDI also provides a range of team-building activities and a book by the principals of the company, Wellins, Byham and Wilson: Empowered Teams. Creating Self Directed Work Groups that Improve Quality, Productivity and Participation (3.5), is a very useful tool for those seeking an overview of the subject.

The rise of learning

Perhaps the most important new contributions to the development of high performing teams arise from Peter Senge's work on learning organizations. Published in the early 1990s, The Fifth Discipline. The Art and Practice of The Learning Organization (3.6) has contributed to the growing interest in providing corporate environments which are attuned to and enable employees to learn. One of the critical elements of such an organization, according to Senge, is Team Learning. Because so much corporate decision making is exercised by teams of people working together, it is important for the team to become a 'learning unit'.

Senge draws rich analogies in basketball and jazz but concentrates much of his advice on the alignment of teams and on the process of 'dialogue'. Dialogue is a team process and consists of a group allowing a free flow of ideas to arise and be discussed. Ideas, even those which are perhaps ill-developed, intuitive or perhaps only marginally defensible are allowed and even encouraged to surface for the group to consider, expand and develop.

The process requires the suspension of immediate judgement until concepts have been collectively explored, built upon, related to the ideas of others and evaluated. The process of discussion and refinement implies a team in which members are at ease with each other, non-combative, mutually encouraging and mutually supportive. There must be an understood egalitarianism and a genuine preparedness to change existingly held views or beliefs.

The pay-off is that the collective interaction of the team will refine ideas and develop them faster, more imaginatively and ultimately more productively than will an individual. This work starts to shed some important insights into the nature or the dynamics of synergy. Furthermore, it offers practical insight into how synergy can be developed and accelerated in a team environment. Although it involves individuals in teams taking interpersonal risks, it is increasingly evident that high performance cannot be achieved without the levels of mutual trust implicit in such risks.

Empowerment and self-directed teams

One of the things that has become increasingly clear as we have learnt more about teams is that high performance is affected by the degree of authority and accountability which is vested in the team.

Within the past few years there has been an increasing interest, and quite a bit of practical application, in empowering teams. The idea rests on the principle of dismantling conventional decision-making systems and nodes of accountability in the organization and redistributing them to teams which are focused on the areas of the business that these decisions most closely affect.

Great success has been achieved in some applications though the extent of change that the organization will undergo as a result is often underestimated. This has occasionally meant that after flirting with the idea, a few organizations have retreated from the commitment, sometimes, it seems, in horror.

Devolved decision making in organizations links back into the way they are structured, how they plan, and what they are doing to achieve responsiveness to change and customer focus. Empowerment of teams is an ingredient, and usually an important one, in the way organizations are seeking to change themselves. It seems that empowerment is an idea whose time has come and lots of people are thinking about it and trying things out.

This brief canter through the history of thinking about high performing teams positions us to look in more detail at how and where teams are used in organizations and, importantly, at how that might change in the future. Almost all the core movements or ideas mentioned above are revisited later in the book and expanded upon in contexts which are relevant to their implementation.

4

How teams are used in organizations – types of teams

This chapter outlines the most common applications of teaming. It shows characteristics of each application and gives examples.

Types of teams

In organizational environments there have traditionally been three common types of team. Each is constituted with differing sorts of members, each operates in differing ways, and each has a specific business use. While there will always be disputes about what to call them, the names I have used probably come close to the most commonly accepted understanding of each type.

The task force

Probably the earliest and in many ways most common team-type activity is when task forces are put together to solve

High Performing Teams

problems. At its worst, this happens when nobody else in the organization can be bothered to deal with the problem – establishing a task force is a good way of getting it off the agenda.

Peters and Waterman do not disclose the name of the company, but they describe in In Search of Excellence (4.1) an organization which had formally created 325 task forces, none of which had completed its charge in the previous three years, and none of which had been disbanded.

Task forces generally operate to solve a given problem. Making them cross-functional means that a number of interests or perhaps operating departments in an organization can contribute to the problem's solution. Sometimes also called Swat Teams, the idea is to hit a problem hard, solve it soon, and find a place or several places where the solutions can be enacted within the organization.

A large number of organizations use this kind of approach. McDonnell Douglas in its defence activities habitually brought together cross-functional groups to solve design problems. Such a group might, for example, consist of a materials scientist, a thermodynamics expert, an accountant and an electronics wizard. The group would be charged with fixing a design problem and doing it fast.

A good and fairly common example of the effective use of the task force was the developing of the Open College's appraisal system. The Open College is an open learning training provider with whom the author worked for some years. A small team was put together to determine best practice and to design the system which would be used. The task force then commissioned the preparation of the training programme which would need to support the appraisal system. Finally the team rolled out the system to the whole staff. Line managers implemented the system, and one year later the task force revised the system to incorporate feedback and then disbanded itself.

Speed is usually of the essence and such teams operate at their best when they can achieve synergy quickly, take fast decisions, minimize bureaucracy, and disband themselves when the problem has been solved. Task forces operate best when there are only a few members, each with sufficient clout in the organization to make commitments.

Quality circles

The Japanese have taught Western business a great deal about using the power of the team to improve the quality of products or services. Quality circles differ from task forces in that their task never ends. In Japan the operating philosophy is based on kaizen; kai means change, and zen means good. That about says it all . . .

Essentially quality circles are there to deliver continuous improvement. This is achieved by teaming people at all operating levels in an organization and focusing them on improvement to both the external and the internal customer. Operators, whether on a production line, in a customer service section, driving forklifts, answering the telephone, or producing the management accounts, have a pragmatic grasp of the possible. Accessing this practical experience and using it to improve operations is the key to successful quality circles.

At higher levels within the organization the need to improve service to internal and external customers is no less pressing than at the coalface. At any level, quality circles function at their best when improvement lies within the immediate ability of the team members to implement. The output of such teams is usually gradualist with incremental improvement driving forward the company's products, services, operations and functions constantly and reliably.

To support quality circles, and for the organization to benefit from their phenomenal contribution, what is required is a company culture which really believes in the power of kaizen. The organization must genuinely listen to its customers and be very aware of its competitors. Above all it must have the humility to realize its vulnerability.

In his riveting book The Fate of IBM, Robert Heller (4.2) describes a visit by Joseph J. Juran, one of the high priests of the quality movement, to IBM's Europe, Middle East and Africa headquarters in Paris. Juran concluded after his day with the company that IBM understood nothing about quality. Within five years IBM's market share had plummeted from 40 per cent to 23 per cent. Heller's contention is that while IBM was saying all the right things about quality, the organization simply convinced itself, based on the evidence of its huge success, that it was providing quality at the top of the industry standard when in fact competitors were providing much higher levels.

J. Edwards Deming, the other great guru of the quality movement, inserts another dimension of difference into the thinking about the type of teaming needed to support quality circles – the dimension of co-operation. Company environments are often internally competitive and that is not necessarily a bad thing. Quality improvement and the effectiveness of quality circles pivot on the ability of the teams to work co-operatively together and to settle their differences in the interest of the customer.

Project teams

The essential function of project teams is to give a future focus for the organization. They are rarely concerned with current operations although their members may have immediate operational responsibility. Often they are set up to develop new and different products or services for organizations. They are sometimes the start of whole new businesses, and sometimes they are simply disbanded because the project is completed or abandoned.

Large organizations invariably have operating divisions which are responsible for existing product lines. This responsibility implies enhancing and extending those product lines within their markets. It may also imply defending those lines against the incursion of others. When the 'others' are within the same organization, it is unsurprising that new products are often torpedoed by existing interests within the organization. One of the responses to this problem is to set up project teams focused on developing a future which is not necessarily a continuation of existing organizational activity.

A mid-sized European bank with which I have worked set up a project team to develop its position in the US markets. The team defined the market segments in which it thought the bank could play. It defined the criteria any acquisition would have to meet in those markets it had identified. Finally it courted, negotiated with and bought a US bank which met the criteria. The team was then disbanded. The process took three years.

In smaller organizations, constituting a project team can imply putting together a group who can open-mindedly look at a future possibly very different from the organization's present. The team will need to gather and evaluate information, and extrapolate a future which possibly integrates some of the existing capabilities of the organization. Usually it will need to evaluate risk, determine critical success factors, create financial models and sometimes engage in full-scale business planning.

These activities should not be confused with an organization's strategic planning function. Setting up a project team is usually a response to an identified strategic opportunity. If it is to work it has sometimes to be protected against any tendency in the organization to kill it off which may happen in much the same way as the body's immune system will attack foreign invasion.

Executive summary

	Task force	Quality circles	Project teams
Purpose	To solve a problem and have the solution implemented in company operations	Continuous improvement of products, services, or company functions and operations	To research and advise on developing new products, services or businesses
Membership	Cross-functional members with 'clout' in their usual operating sectors	Company operatives – people at the coalface, those in touch with customers – at all levels	Visionaries who are also good at business planning and interpreting market research
Tasking	Clear statement of the problem to be solved and an indication of the order of resources available	Broad-based remit to improve all aspects of company functions, products and services	Identification of the project or project parameters plus a clear statement of strategic opportunity the project presents
Time scale	Defined, and as short as possible	Ongoing	Defined – kept under review
Style	Unbureaucratic, fast pace, action orientated	Learning-type style, 're-engineering' approach, customer directed	Research, risk assessment and feasibility type approach
Leadership support	Keep in touch, help anticipate deadlines Legislate in inter-departmental disputes	Help foster and create the TQM culture – 'walk the talk', foster co-operation	Provide access to resources, views, information. Protect against attack from corporate immune system

5

How teams are used in organizations – extending the concept

This chapter outlines the way teaming has developed into broader, more pervasive, applications. It describes why this is happening and shows examples of uses and characteristics of newer kinds of teams.

Extending the concept of teams

These days most organizations have a clear understanding of, and often proven results from, the applications of task forces, quality circles and project-type teams. Many have successfully achieved the increased effectiveness, better use of resources, improved flexibility, creativity and speed of response which they sought in deploying teams in the first place.

Confronting, as they are, a quite different order of competitive environment, almost all organizations have undergone, and quite frequently continue to undergo, wide-ranging strategic change. To survive they have sought to reduce their cost base, improve their quality and levels of service, get closer to their customers, and outwit their competitors by their ingenuity and the speed with which they respond to change.

Unsurprisingly, thinking has emerged which seeks to harness the advantages that teams can provide to the strategic imperatives of a more demanding competitive climate. This has led to a far wider deployment of teams to provide different kinds of organizational resources.

A look at how organizations have used teams to help deal with a new business climate shows that traditional uses have been extended, developed and refined. Three major developments are evident:

- using teams as the building blocks of organizational structure – this is really about **extending the quantity or incidence** of team-based units within the organization;
- deriving greater benefit from cross-functional teams – this is about **extending the scope or range** of organizational functions and processes invested with the benefits of teaming;
- **increasing the authority of teams** so that they become autonomous or self-directed – empowerment. This is about extending the scope of accountability of teams.

We will look at the context and some applications for each of these developments.

Teams as a component of organizational structure – extending the amount or incidence of teaming within the organization

Most organizations are composed of operating departments, and traditionally each department exists because of the common or closely related functions members perform. A job, document or project passes through the department and processes are performed upon it until it passes to another department or eventually is shipped or provided to a customer. Work flows through the department on a basis

High Performing Teams

which still mirrors the production line approach developed in the early part of the nineteenth century.

Functional departments are traditionally aggregated into operating divisions which are again usually based on clustering related functional areas together. This provides the traditional hierarchical organization structure which requires layers of managers first at the head of each functional department, second at the head of each division. Additional layers tended to creep in along the way and this has led us to introduce more hierarchical descriptors like supervisor, first line manager, second line manager, divisional manager, general manager and so on. Our rich language provides ample opportunity for even more gradations and organizations have availed themselves of that richness to an extent which some have recently found an embarrassing cost consequence.

Large and even middle-sized organizations have in the past developed multiple tiers of management which provided a mechanism by which the company could be controlled. These structures also provided the channels of information through which the strategic changes of the organization could be routed, refined and implemented at each operating level. Hierarchical, pyramid-shaped management structures were the norm up until the 1950s.

In geographically dispersed organizations, and most medium to large companies operate from multiple locations, it often became necessary to impose two sets of organizational structures: those required to manage employees located at the site, and those required to provide the continuity of functional management. For example, the finance people at locations A to Y had still to be accessible to the management control of the central finance operation which was located at Z.

This led to the development of matrix management – an employee having both an operational reporting line and a different functional, or sometimes even professional, reporting line. Matrix management also sought to deal with one of the great limitations of functionally based organizational structures. This is called the silo effect: the tendency for the members of a department or division to focus so completely upon internal criteria that the overall purpose of the department, its service to customers or to other operating units within the organization, becomes neglected or forgotten.

Some of the negative effects of these cumbersome, unresponsive structures seriously affected the competitiveness of organizations. As late as the 1970s we had motor car manufacturers designing cars without reference to their manufacturing divisions. This led to increases in internal manufacturing costs because designers could not or would not work in tandem with manufacturing units to optimize the design/manufacturing cost compromises. Designs were not even necessarily based on driver preferences, but rather on 'out-featuring' the competition. This meant that the more inwardly focused companies lost market share as customers sought the cars of manufacturers who were designing them more in tune with their needs and preferences. The great battle of US gas-guzzlers versus Japanese compacts in the 1960s and 1970s is a classic example of what happens when multiple tiers of powerful managers protect their turf.

Balancing the relative power and influence of the organizational silos also deflected companies from their real purpose in serving their customers. We have the example of the banks during the early 1980s. Traumatized by the effects of bad lending decisions in the past and confronting the need to make record provisions, they strengthened the control of central lending departments across all operations. This certainly led to an improvement in the quality of lending and reduced bad debt provision, but it also brought about a decline in market share as other kinds of financial institutions eroded the edges of the banks' traditionally loyal markets.

As it has become necessary to shed operating overheads, organizations have increasingly looked at the cost of multiple tiers of management controlling sometimes internally competitive silos and have moved towards the flatter organizations with which we are now more familiar. This has meant reducing the number of layers of seniority within organizations, bringing the top and the bottom closer together. Balancing the power of competing divisions within the organization has also guided thinking as to how the organization should be organized and structured.

Organizational redesign has been influenced too by the falling cost and improving performance of information technology; the chairman can talk directly to bottom-rung employees. More importantly, the organization's key operating information – customer records, inventory information,

High Performing Teams

prices and specifications of products etc. – can be readily and accurately accessed by anybody within the organization.

A route that many organizations have chosen is to reframe the activities of their functionally based operating components by organizing them into teams. While the organizational structure may not have significantly changed beyond the elimination of management layers, the building blocks of the organization are now teams rather than departments. The intention behind such moves is to access the advantages of innovation, flexibility, speed of response and focus on objectives which characterize the high performing team.

An interesting account of this kind of approach comes from Ron Temple and Robert Droege at Caterpillar in the USA (5.1). Caterpillar, with an international workforce of over 50 000, has increasingly been moving to an organizational design of smaller profit and service centres. One such service centre, located in Peoria, is responsible for, among other things, central purchasing, warehousing, some distribution, transportation and travel, and managing the corporate aircraft. Some 170 people were involved.

Reflecting the thinking behind the reorganization Caterpillar was undergoing, these departments were simply invited to form themselves into teams and focus on two key issues, reducing cost and improving responsiveness to their (internal) customers. Essentially the functions performed by the departments involved were not changed, they were simply converted into teams.

At first the long-serving and experienced managers involved seem to have been cynical of the potential for radically changed performance. They did, however, conduct a number of off-site visits to other organizations which had implemented successful teaming. This seems to have impressed them and been helpful in strengthening their resolve to make the change work.

Fairly soon after being set up the teams insisted that they be allowed to act on and implement the decisions they made as against simply making recommendations which were subject to a manager's sign-off. Here are the seeds of empowerment; one would guess this precondition was critical to their success.

Managers and supervisors who had previously constituted part of the organizational control mechanism were renamed advisers. Their role, as the implementation has progressed, has changed a great deal more radically than the roles of team members. Increasingly they have become facilitators rather than decision makers. Much of their time has to be devoted to removing organizational barriers and reducing excessive procedures. A major part of their new role was the promotion, both upwards and horizontally within the organization, of the whole concept of teaming. It is an interesting, and not very surprising, aside that fewer managers/advisers are required under Caterpillar's team design than was the case in the previous hierarchical organization.

Results have, by and large, proved positive and have enabled staff reductions, improved turnaround times in purchasing, and a general feeling of a smoother running organization. Importantly, employees have been excited; they feel they have substantially changed the way things are done, and plainly they relish the opportunity of delighting rather then merely satisfying their internal customers.

Caterpillar is a case of an organization simply grafting onto an extant structure the benefits provided by high performing teams. A number of organizations in very different areas of business are setting up quite new operations which at the outset use teams as the organizational building blocks.

The great advantage that installing teaming in a greenfield site offers, when compared with the Caterpillar case, is that employees have less unlearning to do before they start relearning again. The inertia which sometimes inhibits the change initiative developing momentum does not have to be overcome. Old hallowed or comfortable practices to not have to be rooted out and eliminated.

Setting up new facilities on the basis of operating teams usually develops great enthusiasm, and experience seems to show that when this kind of approach is used the facility seems to come up to speed faster. This certainly seems to have been the case with NatWest Life (5.2), the assurance arm of the high street bank. It launched itself in 1993, committed to the concept of empowered teams. At the end of its first full year of operation it already ranked twelfth in terms of new business income in the UK and was the largest bank assurer.

A fuller account of such a greenfield site implementation by PepsiCo follows later.

Cross-functional teams – extending the scope and range of processes and functions benefiting from teaming

Counteracting and dealing with the silo effect mentioned above – the tendency for operating units to become too inwardly focused – a number of organizations have extended the application and scope of cross-functional teams. Unsurprisingly this entails creating teams whose members represent different and mixed functional capabilities, and tasking the team to achieve new and different targets. This kind of approach is sometimes taken where benefit is seen in creating a horizontal workflow – i.e. work moving laterally through the organization rather than up and down functional departments (see also 'Business Process Re-engineering', p. 115). Such teams are sometimes temporary, more in the nature of task force or project teams, but increasingly they are being permanently established so that organizational change can be accelerated.

Cross-functional teams are sometimes superimposed on existing organizational structures so that Miss X, a member of the Finance Department (or team), also works with a number of team members appointed from other departments within the organization on, say, a New Product Development team. The advantages of this sort of arrangement are obvious in that the specific functional expertise of each team member will be available to the team so that a better thought-out product will result.

The disadvantages are threefold. First it often makes significant additional demand on the employee's time, and second it can place the employee in a position of divided loyalty between the demands of the team and the demands of the department of which (s)he is a member. The third potential disadvantage is that the team ends up producing a lowest common denominator-type response, that is, they attempt to please or at least appease all interests involved.

What one is looking for is, of course, a highest common factor outcome, one which usually imaginatively satisfies a number of agendas without losing its basic integrity. It means that cross-fertilization of different functions adds

40

value to the outcome rather than simply bending it out of shape – the old chestnut of the camel being a horse developed by a committee.

The customer service team application has become one of the most successful and widely adopted of the cross-functional applications. Here, for example, order taking, invoicing, despatch and credit control might be incorporated into one operating customer service unit. The focus of team members is moved from internal compliance with company procedures to an external consideration of the criteria associated with improving customer satisfaction.

It is frequently the recasting of the core objectives that enables the organization to gain value out of teaming. The focus on a new, different and potentially interesting set of criteria starts to unlock the synergy and provides for team members an excellent context in which they can apply their functional skills. Often it is the realization that an employee develops as to how his/her specific activity relates to corporate intention which enables change and breakthrough. Teaming is a highly effective environment for that relevance to be developed.

The simplicity and obviousness of such corporate moves ignore the radical changes a company has to undergo to achieve them. If, for example, the organization's existing criteria reward falling order processing cost, falling delivery cost, and so on, it becomes a giant leap of faith to substitute a customer satisfaction index as a new key success indicator. Employees having focused upon, been rewarded for, and set objectives to achieve a given condition sometimes find it hard to accommodate a shift which often looks discontinuous with the past. The reality is that old and new sets of indicators often run hand in hand until either the leap of faith is justified or the duality of purpose becomes unsustainable.

Besides the application of cross-functional teaming within the customer service area, the concept has had considerable impact in manufacturing, and we will see some examples of this in the following chapter. It also remains the primary method by which quality circles and hence continuous improvement initiatives operate.

Moving from a functionally based organization to such a cross-functional team approach often generates additional expense for the organization, and only some of it may be evident at the planning stage. The evident part might be the investment in plant or facility layout, IT and telecommunications, the cost of moving staff around, training and so on.

The less evident part is the opportunity cost that implementing cross-functionality can generate. It is rare that the transition happens without disruption. Sometimes it produces initial staff dissatisfaction, often there is a dip in productivity. What is evident from most organizations going this route is – the now often repeated rondo – that the pay-off takes longer than anticipated.

Self-directed teams – extending the authority and accountability of teams

The third major extension of the teaming concept arises both as a reason for and as a consequence of a team earning the 'high performing' descriptor. During the process of a team coming together members will assess the limitations that surround its activities and will usually seek to broaden the team's power base. In fact teams almost always challenge the framework in which they are asked to operate, and the team's sponsor or manager will usually be drawn into a renegotiation. In the Caterpillar case mentioned above, the service teams negotiated the autonomy to act on the decisions they took rather than simply make recommendations.

But the vision of the self-directed team is broader than the kind of turf negotiations which always go on as teams are created. The things which distinguish it are:

■ The team takes over a whole process or multi-functional activity, it allocates the flow of work itself, and frequently it deals directly with suppliers and with customers.
■ It sets its own targets and takes responsibility for achieving them; these targets are usually qualitative and quantitative.
■ Leadership within the team is often shared, sometimes revolving among members; decision making is consensual and responsibility for decisions is shared.

In other words it operates as a mini-business within the organization. The much-brokered word is **empowerment** –

How teams are used – extending the concept

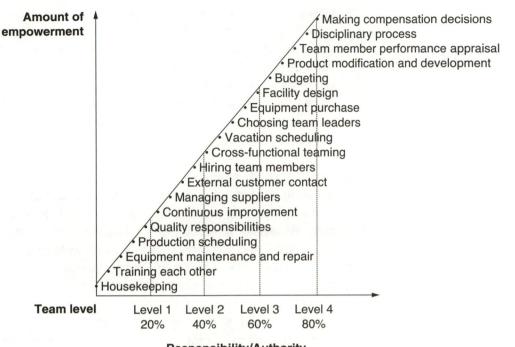

Amount of empowerment

- Making compensation decisions
- Disciplinary process
- Team member performance appraisal
- Product modification and development
- Budgeting
- Facility design
- Equipment purchase
- Choosing team leaders
- Vacation scheduling
- Cross-functional teaming
- Hiring team members
- External customer contact
- Managing suppliers
- Continuous improvement
- Quality responsibilities
- Production scheduling
- Equipment maintenance and repair
- Training each other
- Housekeeping

Team level

Level 1	Level 2	Level 3	Level 4
20%	40%	60%	80%

Responsibility/Authority

devolving upon the group the authority and the means which will enable them to accept accountability for their actions.

Perhaps one of the most revealing models of empowerment is that of Wellins, Byham and Wilson, which is reproduced with permission. In their important and much referred to Empowered Teams: Creating Self Directed Work Groups that Improve Quality, Productivity and Participation (3.5), their model shows how a team might increase the scope and nature of its activities, usually over a period of time, until it becomes an **autonomous** (and that is the other much-brokered word) team.

A moment's reflection will surface two important consequences of the route to and function of self-directed, empowered or autonomous teams.

- ■ They are pretty well incompatible with hierarchical organizational structures. Such structures vest levels of authority at different levels or layers within the organization, and functions are vested in departmental cells. A self-directed work group will usually operate across an increasing number of functional cells and it will also seek to subsume the authority exercised by people at more senior levels within the organization.

High Performing Teams

■ Ultimately these teams must report in, and this will be to a 'manager' of some kind even within a flat organizational structure. The role of that manager, what (s)he actually does, is going to have to be radically different from traditional or even enlightened managerial experience. (A client of mine rejects the manager-as-coach or manager-as-facilitator descriptors, insisting that manager-as-gopher more accurately describes the role.)

The great account of an organization's transition from traditional hierarchical structure to an aggregation of self-directed (or autonomous, or empowered, or all three) teams is Ricardo Semler's Maverick! (5.3). Because of Semler's engaging style, and the restless iconoclastic personality that shines through it, this book is an often hilarious account of organizational transitions which are deeply serious in their consequence.

Semler inherited the family firm which is a diversified medium-tech. manufacturer, and within short order fired most of the existing top management. The book tells the story of how the company was rescued from the brink and brought slowly to health. It then goes on to chronicle first how size led them to split the organization and then how self-directed teams, initially manufacturing cells, took hold in the company and, by expanding the scope of their activity and the levels of their authority, have propelled Semco to becoming the fastest growing company in Latin America. Chapter headings like 'When the Bananas Ate the Monkeys' and 'The Inmates Take Over the Asylum' give a flavour not only of the style of the book but also of how radical were the changes the company has undergone.

Towards the end of this book we return to the need to sell the idea of empowered teams upwards in an organization. We need not labour the pro and contra argument here, but it is important to make clear that most organizations do not find it easy to relocate the locus of decisions. For those, usually middle managers, losing the right to take those decisions, we know it to be threatening. For senior managers, vesting accountability in a new and untried collective entity such as a team can be equally threatening especially when, as has usually been the case, an existing manager is doing a fair job at it anyway.

In summary it is clear to see that organizations are:

■ enlarging the traditional deployment of teams to be an adjunct to the way an organization is structured;
■ expanding the advantages of cross-functionality to add value to processes;
■ devolving more power upon teams to develop empowerment.

All of these responses are aimed at creating a different sort of organization; essentially one that is more responsive to changes in strategy, to changes in the customer base served, and to changes in the external environment.

After the executive summary we go on to look at some applications.

Executive summary

Extending . . .	. . . The incidence of teams in an organization	. . . The scope or breadth of teaming	. . . The authority and accountability of teams
Application	• Teams used as the units of organizational structure	• Greater use of cross-functional teams	• Creating: – Self-directed teams: – Autonomous teams – Empowered teams
In response to	• Downsizing, delayering • The opportunity of falling cost of IT	• Cumbersome unresponsive organizations • Inward focus – silo effect • Process re-engineering	• Need to change the locus of decision making • Providing empowerment, a key ingredient for high performance
Purpose	• Improve focus on objectives; improve flexibility and speed of response • Faster start-ups of greenfield operations	• Move focus from meeting internal objectives to external needs • Improve quality of decision making through broader participation • Accelerate change	• Create mini-businesses • Accelerate change
Consequential effect	• Changed managerial role to – adviser, facilitator – removing organizational barriers	• Redefinition of success criteria is needed • Organization structure has sometime to be altered radically	• Requires completely re-structured organization • Manager role radically changed . . . • Manager as gopher

6 Some applications and experience

This chapter indicates the range and scope of applications to which teaming has been put. It shows a number of examples illustrated by case reports. It describes some of the experience others have had as a result of implementing teaming applications. It also looks at a couple of failed attempts and narrates some consultants' experience of implementation.

Introduction

Having looked at the three generic types of teams and then at some extensions of the teaming concept that organizations are attempting, it will help if we look at some applications organizations have employed and the experience they have had.

Obviously the range and variety of uses to which organizations have put teams is literally countless. In a recent survey of 100 UK organizations using teams, almost all respondents expected to expand their use in the future. US and UK surveys seem to indicate that project teams – usually limited-life problem solvers – are still the most frequently used form but there also seems to be rapid growth in permanently constituted teams. Surveying the main reasons organizations adduce for setting up teams shows characteristically different transatlantic attitudes.

Wellins, Byham and Wilson (3.5) in the USA cite the following reasons in descending order of importance: quality, productivity, cost reduction and job satisfaction. There data are taken from a survey of DDI customers.

An IRS Employment Review (6.1) conducted in the UK in 1995 cites winning greater co-operation, culture and attitude change, improved problem solving and improved project management as major organizational motives for implementing teaming.

It is fair to say that not only are these two surveys very different in nature but they were also conducted some time apart. Nonetheless most managers will identify with both the US and the UK motives. They are organizational objectives likely to be on the agenda of any modern organization, public or private sector.

At best it is possible to convey only a flavour of the diversity of applications to which organizations are applying teaming solutions. In selecting appropriate case reports I have used three criteria:

■ The application addresses an organizational need which is likely to be quite widely felt.
■ The particular form of the application seemed highly appropriate to the organizational purpose it was supposed to address.
■ I have also looked for the case to add an additional interesting dimension, experience or insight.

Product/service design and development

One of the imperatives of the new business climate is the need to accelerate the product development cycle. Products and services have to be brought to the market with shorter gestation periods, often because of the pressure of competitors, sometimes because the windows of opportunity for them are relatively brief. In most cases too, product life cycles are getting shorter and this means that product improvements and product extensions must be accelerated as well.

Cross-functional teams have shown demonstrable superiority in accelerating new product development. If the stakeholders in the product – designers, manufacturing, marketing, selling, maintenance, shipping, finance etc. – are capable of working as a high performing team, significant competitive advantage can be gained by bringing products and services from the drawing board to the client more quickly and with fewer launch glitches.

It hardly needs spelling out why this is so. Because the team is accessing, at source, the good up-to-date information which its members have, it is unlikely to design a product or service that will hit snags in any of the organization's functional activities. Time will be saved by not having to 'sell' the project internally. Or probably more accurately, the new product will have many more enthusiastic sales people, the members of the team, to make the internal sale. Finally, participation in the development will probably have engendered the excitement, commitment and buy-in from members to help make the product fly.

It is also probably true that a cross-functional team will generate greater creativity and innovation in designing the product. Experience shows that if the organization is to access team imagination, however, creativity must be a criterion in the team's charter. The organization must not only convey the expectation of innovation, it must also be prepared to live with the consequences. It is quite proper to vest in the team the accountability for the success of their inventions, but then the organization must also be prepared to accept a measure of failure and the team must have the right to make mistakes.

What is certain is that if the organization strangles all of the team's innovative products at birth, that creativity will pretty soon dry up and the team will opt for the safe solution. There must be a relationship between the degree of empowerment vested in a product development team and the quality of creativity accessed as a result. I know of no studies which purport to measure this, however.

British Telecom

48

British Telecom (BT) Apparatus Division must represent one of the largest and most purposeful applications of cross-functional teams employed in product development. By BT standards this is a relatively small part of the business, representing only about £1 billion of income per year! Apparatus was not profitable to BT in 1993/4 but the division is seen as important since for most users the apparatus is what BT feels like and looks like. It is the gateway through which the diversity and versatility of the network (which we do not see, but where the real money is made) is delivered.

BT's product teams were tasked with the need to develop products which would reinforce the BT brand, make the use of the network easier, and make money. Complete responsibility rested with six cross-divisional teams for developing, launching, managing and maintaining, and finally, withdrawing and disposing of apparatus. Additionally product teams needed to conform to the ISO9000 quality standards. Sourcing was international.

Product development teams were set up with members drawn from a range of operating divisions within BT and each member had to give of their best in the team environment on the one hand, and on the other, to negotiate the support of the divisions of which they were a part.

In the event, the product teams were able to steer the apparatus business back into profit during 1994. They also managed to do so while continuing to operate in BT's matrix-type organization, and in an environment which had only recently sustained the trauma of moving from monopoly to deregulation.

In reporting BT's experience Adam Scott (6.2), a former Director of the Chairman's office, suggests that it was not easy to create and maintain team objectives within the complex BT environment. His judgement from the experience though is that getting clear about the objectives is critical to success. Supporting teams with the mutual trust and commitment necessary to meet objectives also proved difficult.

Much as the logic of cross-functional teams recommends itself for product-service design and development, there is research that strikes a cautionary note. Ranney and Deck in 'Making Teams Work: Lessons from the Leaders in New Product Development' (6.3) find clear evidence that companies that are more successful at introducing new products use their teams differently from those that are less successful. Among the things successful companies do are:

■ They maintain team continuity from concept to market introduction.
■ They review team composition so that the most appropriate people are on the team at each stage.

High Performing Teams

■ They associate membership and leadership of new product teams with success in their organizations.

This research implies that the organization cannot simply dabble in teaming; it must show a significant level of commitment to the concept, and the team itself must optimize its membership and activities to achieve high performance.

A final important contribution from Ranney and Deck indicates that while major new products benefit from high performing cross-functional teams, simple product improvements and extensions can probably be more effectively achieved without recourse to the team.

Manufacturing applications

Volvo

The building of Volvo's Kalmar plant in the 1970s was probably the most significant manufacturing event since Henry Ford laid down the first production lines early in the twentieth century. At Kalmar, semi-completed cars are moved around the plant, which was especially designed for the purpose, and teams of workers build and install complete systems, e.g. the electrical wiring or the transmission train, into the car.

The effect was amazing: a massive 25 per cent decrease in production cost of cars and a steadily improving level of build quality.

Volvo's motive in pursuing this course of action was not declared as reducing the cost of production; Per Gyllenhammar, the president of Volvo, described the purpose as helping employees 'find meaning and satisfaction in their work'. One would have thought that this concept of team-driven cell manufacturing would, on Volvo's results, whatever the company's declared motives, have spread through heavy manufacturing like a forest fire. It did not, and the manufacturing focus of the 1970s and early 1980s was on automation.

Automation of itself helped enable the creation of flexible manufacturing systems. Advanced manufacturing technology, robotics, intelligent storage, retrieval and transport systems all helped to minimize the tyrannical linearity of the production line to favour the work cell philosophy. It was as if having achieved the performance improvements through the investment in hardware, the focus came back to the potential for performance improvement through investment in people.

While simultaneously taking a tilt at F. W. Taylor, one of the champions of production line-based work study, Ricardo Semler (5.3) provides a simple and compelling description of how Semco's marine products division organized itself into work cells. The 120 employees of the division, who were all involved in the selection of a new factory site, proceeded to lay out the plant providing clusters of machines necessary for the complete manufacture of given products. Team members learned to operate all machines in the cluster and any other activity necessary to support it, e.g. driving a forklift between store room and machine cluster. The team then manufactured the product from start to finish and became accountable for quality.

Going into greater depth on the nature and operation of manufacturing cells or teams, two case reports illuminate important practice. The first outlines the use of rewards to achieve organizational goals. It arises from the research of Terry Besser at Iowa State University and covers researches he has conducted at Toyota's Camry plant in Kentucky (6.4). The second deals with continuous improvement at a Boeing subsidiary in Oregon (6.5).

The Toyota rewards case

Besser's research sought to establish the ways in which Japanese management techniques have been transported into offshore operations and to test their effectiveness.

The Toyota plant was a greenfield site, originally commissioned to operate with some 3000 employees building 240 000 Camrys per year. The plant is not unionized and it is now staffed overwhelmingly with American nationals. More than 80 per cent of the employees are organized into teams and, barring some slight differentials based on length of service and job category, all team members earn the same with the team leader earning some 5 per cent more.

High Performing Teams

The operating philosophy which Toyota has inculcated into the plant is a concept described as 'Community of Fate'. This implies that employees believe that what is good for Toyota is good for them. In a broad sense employees must perceive their company as well run, successful and expanding. Links must be made between 'my efforts as an individual' and the results that the organization is achieving. The Japanese company reputation for lifetime employment is regarded by employees as overwhelmingly important. While no formal agreement on this exists between Toyota and its staff, it is believed that working very hard during the good times will lead the company to 'look after me' during the bad times.

The philosophy of community of fate is implemented by interposing team membership as the intervening node of association. Paying all members of the team roughly the same promotes feelings of equality and at the same time helps bond employees together in their primary relationship with their immediate work colleagues. Equal pay helps develop a sense of interdependence which leads each member of the team to perform in support of colleagues; it also leads the team members to surface and address substandard performance of individuals.

The team covers itself internally for illness, holidays and other absences. Interestingly, a culture has developed that members come on duty fifteen to thirty minutes before the start of a shift to ready themselves.

When Toyota pays a bonus, money is allocated to the team, not individual employees. The company also runs a system of rewards for suggestions for continuous improvement. In such cases the team is awarded gift vouchers – vouchers rather than cash because this means that individuals acquire a tangible object, one in which their family often shares, in recognition of the suggestion; every time this object is viewed its genesis is recalled. 'Personal Touch' money is also available to teams to be used for minor social purposes the team may wish to organize.

Toyota's teams are small, four or five people, and this provides more opportunity for promotion to a team leader role. Before such promotion occurs the new leader is required to attend training courses of two hours a day for up to six weeks – this takes place in the employee's own time. A trip to Japan usually results as well. The larger than usual

52

opportunities for promotion, coupled with the seriousness of training involved, help further to foster the community of fate ideology.

It is interesting that Toyota's employees see themselves as working extremely hard and those who have left the company often cite this as a reason for leaving. Toyota espouses a company philosophy which seeks to minimize waste. This embraces materials, processes, systems and employees. It is part of the community of fate philosophy that having the bare minimum number of employees will enable the company to continue to keep them all aboard when the hard times occur.

In the Toyota case we see the organization substituting the unit in which the performance improvement is sought from the individual to the team. Most organizations, including those which avow teaming, focus management time on the performance of individuals. This means that managers deal with performance shortcomings and with simple disciplinary activities like tardiness etc. Remuneration, including bonus or incentive payments, is also associated with individual performance. Recognition too is usually focused on the individual rather than the team.

Toyota seeks to deal with individual performance and disciplines at the team level, but to bond the teams to the overall organization ethos and culture. The effectiveness of the team in controlling and directing individual behaviour is enormous. When team performance is the unit of measure and the unit of reward, the internal dynamics of the team will assure high performance among members.

It is a measure of success that the Kentucky plant runs on a significantly lower fixed employment base than do comparable plants. It is also true that employees' sense of belonging appears to be strong, but whether to Toyota or to their team is not clear. The downside, as reported by those who have left the company, is that their leisure time and time with their families was seriously affected by how hard they worked.

By these former employees, Toyota seems to have been seen to ask too high a degree of employee commitment for the chimera of protection offered by the community of fate philosophy.

The Boeing productivity case (6.5)

Based in Corinth, Oregon, this Boeing plant assembles parts of Boeing aircraft which are then shipped to other sites where the company's aeroplanes are built. The workforce operates in a series of teams and the culture of the plant is focused on continuous improvement. The case has significance in that Boeing has built in the operating systems to support the practice of continuous improvement and has succeeded in making it systemic within the organization.

At the heart of the system is a planning document which is called the Oregon Productivity Matrix, 'Oregon' because it was devised by Oregon State University Productivity Center. Essentially the document isolates a number of categories of measurement: Administration, Safety, Quality, Scheduling and Cost. Each of these in turn is broken down into two or three component parts which provide for the whole organization a mutually shared definition of the constituents of productivity within the plant.

Teams meet to assess their performance against this document. They also establish a series of goals within these categories of measurement which reflect members' collective views of where they need to improve. The structure of the document is such that an overall index of performance can also be calculated by allocating weights to the main areas of measurement. Weighting also enables the team to establish those areas which are of special importance.

Establishing the goals inevitably triggers a detailed discussion of how they will be achieved, the action plan for doing so, the time scales over which it might be possible and so on. This discussion, and the team's increasing proficiency in using the system, is seen as key in developing the team members' ownership of the goals they are trying to achieve.

Goals are usually established over a quarterly time frame, but performance against them is calculated weekly and the results are plotted against a graph which is posted in public view. Once a goal has been achieved it becomes the base line or norm of the team's performance. The team then goes on to address another area of performance, and if the norm it has established earlier starts to slip, the team will know it and rectifying it becomes part of the goal setting and action planning.

Some applications and experience

Boeing does not use these performance measures in any way to promote competition between teams, nor does it reward performance against achieving goals. The system is seen as more important for providing the basis of the dialogue needed to plan, set goals, take ownership and measure.

It seems that the achievements of Boeing's Corinth plant show two significant strengths:

- A common denominator of measurement has been established, and the organization accepts the validity of its components. The data needed to support the measurement are also available and, moreover, available weekly, thus providing the team with excellent feedback loops.
- The participative dialogue of objective setting serves team members in orientation, aspiration and contextual understanding of the organization's business.

Customer service applications

It is a characteristic of contemporary business that customers are becoming increasingly demanding. Serving customers better is a constant catch-up activity for most organizations, consistently trying to exceed their competitors' levels of service. Regrouping into a single customer inter-face team a series of activities which are relevant to the customer, but may be dispersed within different operating divisions of the organization, is an increasing response to service improvement.

Roberts Express

Roberts Express, a 50-year-old US freight carrier, reports in Best Practice UK (6.6) the story of their transition to CATs, customer assistance teams. The organization has plainly always had a strong customer focus and as it grew, regularly conducted satisfaction surveys which started to indicate that customers were experiencing a sense that the service they were receiving was becoming depersonalized. There also appeared to be an increase in error rate and signs of break-downs in communication with customers.

Roberts saw CATs as the solution but decided to start out with a pilot team of seven people all selected for their interest in teaming. Each came from a different functional department within the organization and together they represented the main operating divisions of the company. The team sought to handle the entire process of interaction with the customer: taking the customer's phone booking for a collection, despatching transport, informing the customer of collection time, monitoring and assuring delivery – the whole cycle in fact.

Success with the pilot team lead to a wider implementation within the organization. A computer system had to be redesigned and managers started to sell the idea across the organization. Resistance was immediately encountered from supervisors who were fairly uncomfortable with a new role as 'expert resources and facilitators'. Potential team members too were resistant to change.

At the time of reporting Roberts had 26 CATs of seven to nine people in operation, each focused on a given geographical area. Members are encouraged to try all roles within the team and to develop a speciality in one. Employees take proficiency tests as they move up through a graded ranking system, this affects base salary.

A managing by objectives (MBO) system which had previously been in effect has been extended to incorporate the new organizational design. Criteria are highly quantifiable, e.g. telephone response time, customer satisfaction indices etc. This MBO system also determines the bonus which will be paid.

Roberts Express' experience in implementing this approach is fairly typical. Any conversion to teaming will inevitably challenge traditional hierarchical structures, and resistance at a supervisory level is not uncommon. Employees are usually also wary about any changes in structure, especially when this may mean different immediate colleagues, altered criteria of performance measurement and, probably most important of all, potential difference in pay and other forms of compensation.

Differing from the example of Roberts Express is the experience of organizations which deliver complex process-based services to customers. The difference lies in the variety and range of services and activities such organizations must focus on the client interaction. Such services often require a level of customizing, tailoring or mutual adaptation; consultancy services are an excellent example, as are some customized IT applications.

The standard means of providing such services has been on a case management basis. This means that usually a single individual in the supplying organization is responsible for mobilizing and project managing the delivery of the required services. This is achieved by the 'case manager' interacting with a number of specialist departments in the supplier organization, multiple briefing, multiple pleading and usually multiple opportunities for disaster!

Open College

The Open College provides in-house training and development to corporate clients and specializes in open learning delivery. Completing a management course leading to, say, a Certificate in Management can take a year, during which time a number of ongoing activities must be managed in the College's relationships with clients. These start with making the corporate sale, agreeing and customizing the content and assessment systems the programme will use. Implementation implies delivering open learning materials, providing tutorial support, organizing workshops and dealing with learner assignments. Quality control is exercised through a number of steps which assure compliance with the clients' criteria and conformity with the Awarding Body's standards. Commercial considerations of invoicing, warehousing, cash collection etc. also bubble along in the background of this extended relationship.

The only sensible way to manage this multi-functional relationship is to create a team which is responsible for all aspects of the client relationship. An important member of that team is the client.

Just as purpose is vital in determining the activity and responsibility of all teams, so is it necessary in this extended client/supplier relationship for a clear and unambiguous purpose to be developed, objectives to be established and criteria to be agreed. It is also important that the team meets, with agreed agenda, assesses, problem solves and even brainstorms if necessary.

More development work needs to be done in forming teams between suppliers and clients. It may be that the difference in motives and agenda between them may never allow for high performance to develop in the sense that it unlocks the synergy of a totally co-operative team environment. The prospect looks an attractive area to try to develop, however.

A public service application

In converting many UK government departments into agencies, the government sought, among other things, to develop new ways of working which might draw on appropriate aspects of Civil Service practice and also on the rather different work practices of the private sector. The new agencies looked for both economies of operations and improvements in customer service. To help codify the latter the Citizen's Charter system was evolved which laid out the basic rights of a person in dealing with one of the new agencies and hence defined the minimum levels of service each would have to provide.

Among these new organizations is the Benefits Agency, and the case which follows is interesting for a number of reasons:

- It is a public service application in an Agency staffed with civil servants when it was set up.
- It shows how an organization can dip a toe in the water to test teaming – and what might happen as a result.
- It is an application which has been driven far more purposefully by employees than by management.

The particular branch of the Benefits Agency in the North West has for some while been involved in an empowerment training programme. This appears to have been an important precondition to the events which followed for it had at least opened people's minds to forms of working which are radically different from traditional hierarchies.

Molly, the supervisor of the telephone enquiry service, left, and it was decided that the group should try its hand at being a self-managed team. Eight women are involved in the team, mostly part-timers. The team handles 4000 phone enquiries per month and provides advice on Severe Disablement Allowances, Maternity Benefit and Incapacity Benefit. Its enquirers are the public, employers, other benefit sectors and welfare departments.

A 'boundary manager', Sue, was appointed when Molly left in July and the agreement was that the team should run itself and call for Sue if they got into trouble. The experiment would be reviewed in October. Sue's commitment of time to the team is now half an hour every four weeks, formal review time every six months and being accessible. The call on her accessibility has declined steadily since inception.

Initially the team interpreted their new-found egalitarianism in terms of each of them having to do the same job. Fairly rapidly they came to the conclusion that they could use individual strengths as the core of functional specialism. They also found that without a supervisor to whom to take difficult cases, they needed to develop their knowledge background in order to deal faster with clients and to provide the enquirer client with a 'one-stop shop'.

They have not only greatly increased their base of knowledge, but they have also instituted a system of continuous analysis of the incidence and nature of their enquiries. Frequently an enquirer needs advice on forms of benefit which are the province of other departments within the Agency. Having identified Income Support as one such candidate, they have equipped themselves with the necessary resource materials to deal with these enquiries, they have trained themselves on the different help screens which service such enquirers and they are getting current on the detailed information related to the benefit. They have instituted a customer satisfaction survey in addition to that conducted by the department so that they can measure customer satisfaction for their specific team.

They have established an overall reduction in calls as the key criterion for success. This has led them to analyse reasons for calls. By identifying two major reasons, they have sought to solve the problems these calls represented at source. Realizing that changes in unemployment-related benefits would generate more enquiries, they have persuaded Job Centres to stock incapacity claim forms and they call Centres regularly to check stock and replenish.

High Performing Teams

Part-time work means that these women do not often meet together regularly and hence communication between them all is a problem. They have initiated a Communication Book in which they record messages and ideas, and they have equipped themselves with a whiteboard to record more immediate information.

They have not found the assumption of responsibility easy, but their achievements have made them extremely satisfied. They see themselves as 'driving change rather than being driven by change'.

Others within the office have questioned the creation of what is seen as an elite team, but the department of some 60–70 people in which this team is located is now moving to implement a far wider base of empowered teaming. Fundamental to the thinking is the need to eliminate the current supervisory structure and substitute a system more attuned to the work flows within the department. Parallel to this, training and development on empowerment continues with the result that communication within the department and constructive confrontation have improved immeasurably.

If the detail of what this team has done seems to be exhaustively reported, it is included to show the ingenuity and originality which can be accessed if the team is empowered to do it. It is also important to remember that this team has no leader. It is perfectly conceivable that an energetic supervisor might have been able to develop the same enhancements and improvements in the traditional manner of hierarchical organizations. I would lay money on the fact that it would have taken longer, however, and, as is the case with introducing most change in the working environment, it would have been accompanied by a great deal of kicking and screaming.

Some notable changes in function

In the discussion on using teams as the organizational building blocks, we looked at the experience of a group of Caterpillar's service departments incorporating the benefits of teaming into an existing organizational structure. This case reflected a relatively unchanging role for the departments involved. This is not always the experience of organizations which commit to, set up and empower teams.

60

Some applications and experience

Mike Arthur, a personnel planning manager at the Rover Group, recounts the changes in the personnel function at Rover Group Power Train as the company moved from an hierarchical to a team-based structure. Arthur's account is entitled 'Rover Managers Learn to Take a Back Seat' (6.7) and it was originally given at a meeting of the Institute of Personnel and Development.

In the late 1980s Rover eliminated the position of works supervisor and set up a series of work teams with 15 to 20 members called Production Associates; each of these teams has a leader and the leaders report in to a Production Manager.

To facilitate this change Rover sought to empower the team by having its managers devolve a great deal of authority and decision making to teams and team leaders. As we have seen elsewhere, this changes the activity of the manager who becomes a coach, cross-organizational communicator, trainer, agent of development etc.

Rover's line managers now subsume in their repertoire of activity a great deal of what was historically the role of the personnel department, notably in the following areas:

■ Line managers, rather than Personnel, now hire new appointees using a recruitment process designed by Personnel.
■ Training decisions are now taken by line managers and the Personnel Department merely acts in an advisory role.
■ Development of employees is now a line manager role whose responsibility it is to identify high performers.

While worth recounting, all the above is about what one would expect, but it is in the area of industrial relations that the most radical changes have occurred.

Arthur describes that, previously, in a highly adversarial climate of employee relations, the supervisor and/or manager fairly swiftly reached an impasse on any dispute. The employee relations specialist from Personnel then took over negotiation.

Settlement usually involved getting some agreement on some arcane technicality of procedure agreements. As he describes it, the procedure was not only unsatisfactory to all concerned but also alienated managers and employees. One gets the impression of a sort of voodoo going on between shop steward and employee relations negotiator, to the mystification of all but those two and to the haphazard advantage of either the workforce or the company.

The emphasis which has developed on team problem solving, coupled with greater managerial openness, now apparently means that fewer grievances develop into formal procedures and many problems are solved at source.

Underlying Mike Arthur's account are three points on the consequences of adopting a teaming approach, they are all well worth making:

- the changed role of the manager – about which we have been rather repetitious;
- the changed role of the personnel department, from executive to advisory;
- a changed organizational culture, in this case representing a quite different approach to labour relations.

Start-up experience

Converting an existing workforce to a team-based environment, as we have seen in the Roberts Express case, is not necessarily easy. It produces strong reaction, often negative, not only from middle management and supervisory levels within the organization but also from employees. On the face of it, it would seem easier to commission a site on a team basis. There is some evidence that this can be more easily achieved, especially if the process is well thought through.

PepsiCo, in an article entitled 'Come and Be Taken Seriously' (6.8), recount the commissioning of one of their sites, a new Walkers Smiths factory in Coventry. The company's intention was to commission the new plant in seven months rather than the usual twelve and to meet world-class manufacturing performance from the outset. Continuous improvement was also a set of values which the company sought to instil from start-up.

A flat organizational structure was envisaged; team leaders would report to a Plant manager, and all staff would be members of multi-functional teams. To aid the sense of personal empowerment of PepsiCo values, day-to-day decision making was to be vested at the point closest to the work at hand or to the customer.

Some applications and experience

The 'Come and get taken seriously' phrase was used as a headline to staff recruitment advertisements and plainly had the effect of signalling a new and welcome approach because over 900 applications were received.

All eligible applicants were subjected to an applied technology battery of tests to determine verbal, numerical, mechanical and faultfinding aptitude. Candidates whose results justified it then underwent telephone interviewing, designed to assess behavioural indicators of work influence and teamwork. Finally assessment centres were used to determine team attributes and initiative.

New recruits spent two weeks of induction absorbing Walkers Smiths and PepsiCo's values and corporate culture. They were also involved in visiting customer sites with the company's sales representatives, and were required to report back with their findings and suggestions for improvement. Some received technical training in the UK and some at PepsiCo's FritoLay operations in the USA. Finally the whole group spent a week together on team-building exercises.

By any criteria the recruitment, selection, training and induction processes used were comprehensive and should have enabled the company to meet their objectives for the commissioning of the new plant. In general the process seems to have been successful with some interesting lessons.

First it will take longer than anticipated to achieve the multi-skilling to which the plant aspires. The estimate, at the time of the report, is that it would take 18–24 months and that there would have to be a major commitment to training during that period.

The degree of self-direction PepsiCo tried to invest in their teams was not achieved. Some of the group leaders, committed to a high degree of involvement, steered well clear of adopting a directional style. New staff were not necessarily comfortable with this though, and sought a higher degree of leader intervention and assistance with making decisions.

Although this may have been because the plant was new, the experience was that however well prepared people were for highly self-directed roles in theory, day-to-day practice turned out to be different from what was anticipated. PepsiCo feels that the processes started in the new plant must be seen as the first part of a continuum which will need to be sustained by continuous commitment on the part of the corporation and the employees involved.

Top teams

Little research and few accounts exist of successful applications of top teams, the group of people who sit at the apex of the organization and direct its activities. The phrase 'top team' is much used, however, and the implication is that at the top of the organization is a closely knit, synergistic group, with a high commonality of purpose, demonstrating interchangeability of function, imagination and creativity.

Logic would certainly suggest that this condition must exist in many organizations and in fact one might well believe that it was a precondition of success. Experience however does not support the logic. Katzenbach and Smith, two senior McKinsey partners, researching for their book The Wisdom of Teams (6.9), found that a number of things conspired against developing top teams. They cite the deep-seated individualism of senior executives as a reason, and they also suggest that demands on the time of potential top team members may limit or preclude the emergence of high performing characteristics in the accepted sense.

They concluded that the phenomenon, though rare, does exist but is usually confined to very small groups, often partnerships and rarely more than four people. At the same time Katzenbach and Smith suggest that managing major change, as more companies will have to do in the future, is likely to see more top teams emerge.

As if to take up this challenge Allen C. Amason of Mississippi State University has done some interesting work on conflict in top teams and its effect on the quality of decisions taken (6.10). Amason starts with an assumption about the nature and importance of the decisions that top teams take. For ease let us call these strategic decisions; that is, decisions which:

- potentially affect the future of the organization in quite important ways;
- take some time to demonstrate their effect;

Some applications and experience

■ quite often require that the organization enacts change which could be substantial and involve many people.

Getting such decisions right is, plainly, something of a survival issue, and work which explores and identifies successful ways of improving top team decision making is of key importance.

Amason identifies two kinds of conflict:

■ cognitive conflict which is essentially functional, task-directed and focuses on how things should be done;
■ affective conflict which is personal in nature and involves focus on incompatibilities, cynicism, mutual criticism and so on.

Using unimpeachable experimental methods, wide samples and complex statistical analysis Amason then seeks to measure the interplay of these two types of conflict on:

■ the quality of the decisions taken by the top team;
■ the commitment generated among team members to the decision after it was taken;
■ the level of understanding of the decision that members of the team had;
■ the level of acceptance that the team had of the decision.

The results of Amason's studies are quite complicated to absorb, but to simplify and generalize:

■ Cognitive, functionally based conflict seems to improve the quality of the decision, the understanding of the decision and the team's acceptance of it.
■ Affective or personally directed conflict seems to have a negative effect on the quality of the decision and to the acceptance of it as well.

The process of building and developing top teams already is, and will increasingly be, drawing upon these and related findings. If, as many believe, organizations in the future are more likely to be led by top teams whose members provide a range of functional expertise and a broad spectrum of experience, then achieving high performance fast is a pressing necessity.

Specialist teams

Some organizations have created teams in which reposes specialist knowledge, and on which other parts of the organization can draw for advice or help. This sort of application is different from a separate functional department providing services horizontally within the organization. Frequently it is a team made up of members of other departments, functions or teams, which is tasked with developing unique capability within the organization. In some ways it is equivalent to both project teams and task forces though its constitution consciously marks it out as something separate. Such teams are there to provide centres of excellence.

An excellent example of this sort of application is reported by Cliff Bowman and Simon Carter (6.11), the latter a one-time Chief Executive of Baxi Partnership. Baxi is a manufacturer of domestic central heating boilers and heating appliances. As part of a turnaround programme in the early 1990s, Baxi underwent a major structural reorganization, creating a number of strategic business units, each a mini-business in its own right.

Though it is not called a team, a separate group was established called the 'university'. This group pulls together the core knowledge the company requires. It provides knowledge of manufacturing systems, benchmarking, market trend analysis, economic forecasts etc. The university is not responsible for R&D in the sense that new product development falls within the SBUs. It looks further out into the future and provides base data on which the organization can plan.

It does not always work out

Attempts at building teams which 'don't work out' are, unsurprisingly, not well documented in case history. First of all it is hard to define what is meant by 'not working out' because that judgement can only be made in the light of the expectations of the organization when teaming was initiated.

It is perfectly possible to produce welcome and acceptable improvements in productivity, quality or other defined criteria, without ever approaching the synergy characteristic of a high performing team. By calling the unit a team, by requiring it to improve its operations, by causing it to initiate dialogue with its customers and suppliers, and by helping it define and meet objectives for improvement, much can and has been accomplished. Having achieved a level of improvement most organizations would not count the initiative a failure.

Effective teams can operate well below the level of empowerment and well short of high performance. Why it becomes important to aspire to high performance is because such teams achieve breakthrough; they change the game – the order of what they can do is astonishingly beyond normal incremental improvement.

Sometimes, however, the introduction of teaming just does not work.

The Manchester-based plant of the Eaton Corporation, world leaders in truck transmission technology, attempted to introduce self-managed teams in 1981 (6.12). It dismantled its traditional supervisor-based structure, replacing it with teams which exercised, by comparison, a relatively high degree of responsibility. The attempt failed even despite the training and management energy invested in the change. In retrospect, Eaton feel that the plant was simply not ready for the change despite the success the company had had in the USA. The experiment had to be terminated after six months when employees requested a reversion to the original system, preferring to vest part of their autonomy in the person of a supervisor.

Not until some years later, apparently riding on the positive experience of a TQM programme, was Eaton able to re-introduce self-managed teams which are multi-skilled and involve themselves with all aspects of the process from material planning to, in some cases, the successful redesign of machine tools necessary for the process.

At the time this book is in preparation, we are witnessing a struggle at Royal Mail which is as yet unresolved. Royal Mail is one of the best postal systems in the world, with an impressive record of continuous improvement. On a normal day it handles some 70 million letters through 1500 sorting and distribution offices. It meets its delivery criteria in excess of 95 per cent of the time, and it has held its prices for some three years, increasing them only by fiat of its owners, Her Majesty's Government.

High Performing Teams

Royal Mail is attempting to introduce a package of changes within its workforce in which changing working patterns are a key part. The package is a complex one and it is hard, from outside the organization, to assess the merits of the argument which is raging between the management and the union. The management refers to the need to eliminate a series of restrictive practices and, among the means by which it proposes to achieve this, is to organize a substantial part of the workforce into self-managed teams.

Such teams will be expected, among other things, to monitor their own performance, to schedule coverage, taking responsibility for members' absences, and to train and coach new members of the team. They are also expected to meet Royal Mail's quality standards and achieve continuous improvement.

The Communication Workers Union (CWU), the antagonist in this proposed reorganization, protests at the degree of responsibility this devolves upon its members and describes the proposal as 'management-imposed demarcation' (6.13). It further suggests that whereas teaming was originally proposed by the management of Royal Mail as a means to an end, it has now become an end in itself.

It would be wrong to suggest that the resistance of the CWU and the strikes which have resulted are rooted in an objection to teaming alone, for there are other pay- and time-related components in the package. Nonetheless, CWU objection to the imposition of what it calls 'the half-baked dogma that Royal Mail has lifted from American text books on Human Resource Management' is a central feature of the dispute.

Interestingly, this dispute has highlighted the failure of a comparable initiative in the US Postal Service (USPS). Launched as an Employee Involvement (EI) programme in 1982, the USPS sought to eliminate the 'bitter adversarial relationship' which had existed between staff and management. William Bolger, the Postmaster General who launched the initiative, declared that the USPS intended, by the introduction of the EI programme, to meet workers' needs and to recognize their contributions more fully.

In 1995 the USPS unilaterally pulled out of the programme, claiming that national productivity had declined and grievance procedures had increased as a result. The programme was described as not meeting the mutual needs of the USPS or the Letter Carriers Union.

The above cases show us that there can be a wrong time, as in the Eaton case, to introduce teaming. A workforce can also be alienated from the concept if it perceives that the motive for doing so is either misinformed or misrepresented. The penalty of starting out and not achieving success can be long-term alienation.

Why it does not always work out – consultants' and trainers' view

A survey of training practices in the UK indicates that approaching 70 per cent of organizations which are implementing teaming look to outside specialist providers for developing team leaders and team members. Consultants and trainers are then in a position to supply a rich fund of experience and stories. While I cannot pretend to have undertaken a scientific survey of views, in preparation for this book I have talked to a number of colleague trainers and consultants and there is fair uniformity in agreeing the main reasons for teams never reaching high levels of performance.

Members just cannot get on

This looks like the team never really getting to a point where all members share their thoughts, feelings and ideas. At its worst, members snipe at each other, score points, are dismissive or scornful of views, relish indulging in put-downs, and show no mutual respect. Overtly less antagonistic, but equally deadly to the process of team building, is when members simply do not participate fully; they stay on the sidelines, they observe and do not contribute. While this is acceptable, indeed predictable, behaviour at an early stage in team development, if it persists the team will never reach its potential.

There are a number of reasons for this kind of behaviour, foremost among which is that members may have radically different agendas. These can be organizational or personal.

Consultants and trainers will always share the experience of dealing with team members who have been put onto teams to protect an interest elsewhere in the organization.

High Performing Teams

The brief to which the member is working is not about contributing towards the team objective, but rather to prevent department A from taking the high ground from department B. Or it may even be to shed an irksome responsibility of department A's. Sometimes the agenda is straight espionage, keeping a boss posted about what is going on inside the team.

Personal agendas usually have to do with career competitiveness. A member may actually try to capture the control of a team which looks as if it is going to be successful, or publicly dis-espouse membership of a team which looks as if it is going to be in trouble. There are a multitude of ways in which a team can be wrecked by an ambitious or disaffected member. Most of us who have worked on team development have experience in dealing with this.

If the team is weak it may become so demoralized by such tactics that it caves in. If, on the other hand, it is strong and confident, it will turn on wrecking tactics and punish or expel the offending member, often with surprising ruthlessness.

The trick in dealing with the inevitable mismatch with which people come to a new team is to recognize whether the dysfunctional behaviour being exhibited is likely to persist, or whether it is simply a stage in the development through which all teams pass. If it is never going to go away, the team will never perform optimally.

Unclear purpose or objectives

Just as the motives of team members may be confused or may not bear scrutiny, so the motives of the managers in the organizations that create teams are often subject to the same criticism. Consultants probably spend more time working with clients in this area than in any other. What this looks like is the team being really unclear about what is expected of them.

Again, with any new team there is a period when its purpose seems unclear. It needs to be continuously reasserted, usually by the team's manager/sponsor, and usually involves the processes of mission building, developing a shared vision and then resolving these into a set of strategic objectives. Some teams can move through this on their own, some cannot. Some start the process and then find that the manager/sponsor vision is simply too woolly or imprecise. Sometimes the sponsor's declaration of purpose is spurious or flawed. The situation is not unusual and consultants and trainers are often able to contribute.

If the team does not end up convinced of the value, potential and integrity of the purpose, it will never mobilize the energy and enthusiasm to perform. Its activities are likely to be desultory and uninspired and the team will start to atrophy. People will miss meetings, they will not follow through on team decisions, they will plead for reassignment.

in brief. 'It was really clear that he had set us up and sold us a pup. God knows what his motive was, but I wasn't having any. I just fronted it with the team and the only time we actually came together was when we figured out how to get out of the set-up.'
Team Leader

Lack of manager/sponsor support

Trainers and consultants have lots of stories to tell of teams which have got off to a flying start, developed fast and moved into high gear more swiftly than anticipated. They have then hit management resistance, often because they are perceived as posing a threat or simply by requiring too radical a change in the manager's role or authority for him/her to contemplate. The manager believes that (s)he has spawned a Frankenstein monster – the creation is moving out of control.

in
brief

'I felt that I was placed
outside the perimeter
fence and was peeking
in to see what they were
up to at any time.'
'I am really indignant at what
they were suggesting . . . I
really feel they were usurping
my role . . . I am going to
have to slap them back.'
Quotes from managers

Bad team leadership

The leadership inside the team is critical in the early days
of a team's development. A high performing team will be less
reliant on leadership because it will have developed the flexibility to switch roles and functions in response to need.

Leadership that is too assertive, leadership that is too
tentative, leadership that is excessively consultative, leadership that moves at too fast a pace – all these things will slow
a team's development down and sometimes even scupper it.

I believe that consultants and trainers can contribute very
successfully to developing team leaders and teaching them
the behavioural balancing techniques that assist the team's
internal processes and accelerate development. A key
enabler for team leaders is an understanding of the phases
of team development. Each phase requires slightly different
behaviour from the leader, but more importantly, if the leader
can explain to the team what it is going through it will help.

In the next two chapters we look at the steps needed to
set up and develop high performing teams. Doing so
involves anticipating or sidestepping some of the pitfalls
mentioned above – and a great deal more!

What makes high performing teams

This chapter is a brief distillation of the huge range of views which exist on the subject.

What teams actually do to become high performing has, unsurprisingly, been the source of a great deal of observation, measurement, supposition and assorted speculation. Perhaps the reason that no definitive and agreed list of conditions or attributes exists is because while some of the things high performing teams do are measurable and observable, some are not. When members of established high performing teams are asked what it is that has made them successful, their answers fall into five pretty predictable categories.

Purpose

Almost all successful teams talk about clarity of purpose, agreed objectives and knowing where they are going. Successful teams are quite clear about the reason for their existence. They also know what they are there to achieve short-term, which can be different from the longer-term purpose for establishing them. Teams are sometimes set up to achieve a limited set of objectives as a test or pilot to assess whether teaming can provide an advantage for the organization. Either way successful teams seem to know and understand the organization's purpose in creating them. Clarity of purpose obviously facilitates reaching agreement about shorter-term objectives and priorities.

Responsibility and empowerment

Teams which have been accorded a high degree of responsibility will generally derive benefit from a sense of the importance of what they are doing. In Chapter 5 we saw that in the Caterpillar application, the team made it a condition of their charter that they be allowed to act upon decisions they took rather than making recommendations on which others might or might not act. High performing teams are also usually self-directed teams; what they do may be established by their original charter, but how they develop and where they go becomes a matter for the team.

Usually teams move towards assuming increased responsibility as time goes on; we saw a model of this earlier in the discussion about empowered teams. There is a school of thought which suggests that the difference between a team and a simple group of people working together is a function of the accountability vested in the team. I am not certain myself that this relationship is as clear as some would suggest. What is clear is that high performing teams feel – and the organization supports the feeling – that they carry important responsibilities.

Team processes

Successful teams will usually talk of the processes they use to reach decisions. Some of this has to do with the way meetings are conducted, but it has also to do with the sources and quality of information to which the team has access. How they interpret and deal with that information in discussion will also be adduced as a component of success. Teams are usually less clear about what these processes are because they tend to happen intuitively. The evidence is that they equate roughly to the team roles we described earlier: shapers, monitors, evaluators, controllers etc. We return to this subject later in the book in step 9 of 'Setting Up Teams to Achieve High Performance' (Chapter 8).

Team members' contributions

Success will also be described in terms of the contribution of team members; the 'right' people were on the team, the leadership was appropriate, there was a good functional balance of members, person x contributed enormously, and so on. Again we will return to the 'right people' concept in step 5 of 'Setting Up Teams to Achieve High Performance'.

The intangibles – woo woo

There will invariably be a category of success factors which are less tangible. Typical descriptors might be: 'we felt comfortable with each other . . . there was a high degree of mutual trust . . . people were honest with each other . . . people worked well together etc.' Pressed in this area, members will usually not attempt to conceal that disagreements occurred and that differences might sometimes have seemed irreconcilable. Tempers may have been lost and hard words exchanged but a common ingredient of success is that the team developed a mechanism for confronting difference and repairing any damage it caused. Members did not necessarily like one another but it usually turns out that they did respect each other.

It is also important to note that in the conversations about the intangibles, the 'comfort' people felt with each other is not to be confused with members feeling unstressed, at ease or unchallenged. High performing teams learn to cope with stress rather than avoid it.

Helga Drummond in her book The Quality Movement (7.1) refers to the pressure and stress that the Japanese work culture, with its strong basis in teaming, imposes on its employees. She suggests that this is tolerated because of the elaborate social rules which surround interpersonal exchanges, not because people enjoy it or even feel rewarded by it. Similarly, membership of a high performing team is unlikely to be an easy ride though members often do find it very rewarding.

High Performing Teams

If high performing teams are to be created, and if they are to be created quickly, it follows that attention must be focused not only on the hard objective issues, but also on the 'softer' issues of interpersonal behaviour. There is often a reluctance to spend the time examining the soft issues – the touchy-feelies as they are sometimes called. To avoid suggestions of the tactile, I prefer the words 'woo woo', borrowed from Wilson Learning. The evidence is that teams that do confront, deal with and enjoy the woo woo do better than those that do not.

One of the things that also seems to predispose teams to achieve better levels of performance faster is the care and thought which has gone into setting them up. Let us look at the steps that have proven effective. The advice that follows stems from a wide variety of sources rooted both in practical experience and in formal research.

8 Setting up teams to achieve high performance

This chapter suggests a ten-step process designed to guide the manager from first considerations about how to use teams, to a functioning team ready to operate. Though densely packed with advice from many sources there is a strong bias in this chapter to practical experience.

Setting up the team

Step 1 – What is the purpose of the team?

Teams are often set up in response to a perceived organizational problem. It is important to be certain that we know what lies at the heart of the problem we are trying to solve or we might well mis-state the purpose of the team.

Organizations frequently describe difficulties they are encountering in terms which are not problem based but are, instead, statements of the anticipated solution. Immediately this curtails the spectrum of possible solutions and may well lead to courses of action which are based on the ameliora-tion of symptoms rather than the implementation of solutions. Fortunately there are a number of techniques of problem analysis available, and the experienced line manager will need little help in identifying them.

Because organizations are complex, dynamic systems, the presentation of the symptom or the problem needing solution is likely to have a series of interrelated causes, the analysis of which quite often lends a lucidity of definition which changes the approach to solution. In fact if we are not dealing with a complex issue, and one that is likely to be around for the forseeable future, it is rarely justifiable to go to the trouble of setting up an ongoing team to handle it. Rather one would set up a limited-life task force, the purpose of which would be stated quite differently (see the Executive summary in Chapter 4).

Despite the fact that thinking about building teams is usually generated by the organization being presented with a problem it needs to solve, it turns out that in the modern business environment teams are usually set up either to enact longer-term ongoing solutions to repetitive or endemic problems, or to implement a change process.

Whatever the organizational motive, being clear about the problem(s) we are trying to solve enables us to make a statement about the purpose which is intended for the team. As we have seen this is an essential precondition to the success of the team. We will return to the subject when we discuss mission, vision and values later.

Step 2 – Is a team the best solution?

In their punchily written Why Teams Don't work: What went wrong and how to make it right, Robbins and Finley (2.1) make the telling point:

> 'The truth is that teams are inherently inferior to individuals, in terms of efficiency. If a single person has sufficient information to complete a task, he or she will run rings around a team assigned the same task.'

Fred Peters of In Search of Excellence fame on the other hand, a passionate supporter of teams and teaming, would lead us to believe that there are few issues of importance within organizations that would not benefit from team-based solutions.

Setting up teams to achieve high performance

The argument is divided and experience is mixed, as those who have worked with team development in the past will attest. Here is what I hope will be a balanced account of the pros and cons – first the contra argument:

■ Teams take longer to set up than you ever imagine. They need time to 'gel'. They need time to establish their internal relationships. They usually need to create the opportunities for meetings, and just getting members' diaries in synch. will take time. The high performing team rarely 'hits the ground running' though once it is performing well it is likely to move fast.

■ Teams will take a great deal of management support time. Briefing, clarifying, explaining context, negotiating resources etc. all seem to take an inordinate amount of time.

■ Sometimes teams need to be unstuck. If they hit irreconcilable differences, external intervention may be necessary to resolve problems. This might need a manager's intervention or perhaps a facilitator will need to be appointed to get them going again. It can take time while each of the conflicting sub-agendas are dealt with.

■ High performing teams assume a collective responsibility for their decisions and for the actions they take or propose. One of the downsides of shared responsibility in teams that are not performing well is that accountability is disseminated across too many people – nobody carries the can, and this affects the quality of decision taking.

■ If a manager sets up a team and it fails (see Chapter 2), members will not be readily forgiving, and may take some time to get over the difficulties that will have been caused. Failure invariably means that the team must be disbanded before it achieves its objectives. This will, in turn, cause fall-out, recrimination, and loss of confidence. The risks can be high.

The pro argument, the case going the extra distance of setting teams up, is:

■ Cases where a cross-functional approach is a precondition of solving the problem or enacting the changes which will supply a solution obviously support the team case.

High Performing Teams

- If buy-in, commitment to, or ownership of the solution and changes envisaged are an important component of success, a team will help kick-start that process.
- Teams serve a useful purpose in developing people by mixing less and more experienced members. They can also provide an accelerated learning process for everybody involved.
- Sometimes there is a need to change the game in the business environment. In fact let us withdraw the word 'sometimes'. There is a constant need to renew people's interest, creativity, and sense of excitement about what they do. Teaming can provide the additional component of interest and renewal.
- Experience shows that creativity and innovation are more likely to be accessed by a team which is working well. If the problem that needs to solved, or the changes that need to be made, rest on breaking the mould, a team is more likely to achieve that.

Ultimately teams become high performing because, as we have seen above, the woo woo factor works. Anyone seeking to implement a team approach has to ask whether he or she will be able to put together a group where the individuals are vitalized and expanded by working together. Will synergy be unlocked? Well, it is always a gamble, but the intelligent manager who knows his or her people will probably be able to judge the likelihood of success with some accuracy. There is no substitute for gut feeling!

Step 3 – What sort of team will work best?

In Chapter 4 we talked about the three types of teams most common in the business environment:

- the task force – a problem solving team with a defined life expectancy, charged with solving a problem and implementing the solution;
- the quality circle – charged with continuous improvement, an undefined life cycle and an ongoing responsibility;

■ the project team – required to take a longer, future-orien-
tated look at (probably) a strategic change.

Obviously the nature of what needs to be achieved, the
purpose of the team, will dictate what sort of team it will be.
If we are in the more complex realm of using the disciplines
and techniques of teaming to provide organizational strength
and resource – i.e. an extended team concept such as we
outlined earlier – then we need to determine whether we are
ready to support the longer-term implications.

A limited-life, problem solving team theoretically can be
disbanded, but as Dr Frankenstein discovered, it is often
harder to dispense with a lively creation than one might originally have supposed. A longer-term team, one which
becomes a structural component of the organization or part
of the organization's systems, will need to be both constituted and supported in a different way.

A model might look like this:

	Problem solving team deployment	Systemic team deployment
Use	Strategic or tactical, but mostly tactical	Usually strategic – addressed at providing core organizational capabilities
Operating brief	Purpose and objectives	Mission
Life cycle	Usually fixed term	Permanent
Output	Solutions	Ongoing organizational development
Support the manager/sponsor will need to provide	• Provide resources • Protect and defend • Assist with enacting solutions	• Empower • Champion within the organization • Remove organizational obstacles

Step 4 – What will it take to sustain the team within the organization?

Being clear about purpose is critical to structure and briefing, but of overwhelming importance is the degree of
commitment the organization is prepared to mobilize to
sustain teams. Most organizations are not benign institutions

that welcome new initiatives and change. Most have what we have earlier called an immune system. This means new, unrecognized and especially successful intrusions will be regarded as threatening. The organization will seek to defend itself against the unfamiliar and eliminate or neutralize the effect it is causing.

A new, successful and incipiently high performing team might well experience this kind of treatment, and the manager's role is to protect and defend it. Most teaming initiatives are introduced in the middle tiers of the organization, and this means that the manager or sponsor of the team is made busy in selling and defending its activities upwards, downwards, and of course, horizontally as well.

Many managers also find that the change of role that the introduction of a self-directed team can imply is hard to sustain. Moving from the decision maker to the facilitator, from command and control to coaching and counselling, from directing subordinates to developing staff is not an easy transition. Besides the mind shift necessary to sustain the behavioural changes, many managers simply lack the skills, experience and sometimes even the awareness of the necessity to make changes.

It remains a major cause of team failure, however, that the organization renders the team unworkable or that its immediate sponsors fail to support, defend and champion it. Few implementations go without some form of difficulty in the delineation of responsibility and most need to confront differences and renegotiate their space.

We return to this subject in a little more depth in Chapter 13, 'Other Important Things to Think About'.

Step 5 – Who should be appointed to the team?

As a general axiom, remember that the larger the team the longer it takes to hit form. Also large teams usually work more slowly than small teams. If meetings are a process that the team is to use – and for most teams they are – arranging them in the busy times we live in will further slow things down.

Setting up teams to achieve high performance

So the lesson is to go for the smallest number of people you can, compatible, of course, with two other considerations: eligibility and suitability. The interplay of these last two factors comes from our friend Belbin of whose work we read earlier in Chapter 3.

Eligibility

This rests on the experience, training, background and current position or function of the potential member. For example, in a team where cross-functional membership is important, an eligible member would be someone from one of the departments involved who knows how that department operates, is probably experienced in more than one of its activities, may have been there for a while, and possibly has some clout in the department. Eligibility borders on the idea of the 'right' to be a member of the team.

Suitability

This falls more in the area of being able to make some positive contribution to the unique or new purpose for which the team is being created. Examples here might be that the person has shown creativity or a capacity for innovation, has demonstrated ability to work on teams in the past, or might be a good external communicator. Suitability rests more on the qualities, nature or capabilities of the potential member and how aligned these are with the intention behind setting up the team.

Plainly neither dimension can be ignored. The criteria for eligibility will be self-evident. The good news is that there is both an excellent body of research to support the components of suitability, and also the means, through psychometric measurement, to determine the existence of those qualities in candidate members of the team. In other words, we can predict the probable behavioural contribution any potential member will make to the processes of the team. To understand this more fully we need to look more closely at the team roles Belbin's work has provided for us. Those that follow are taken from Team Roles at Work by R. Meredith Belbin 1993 (3.2), a book whose printing history attests to the wide and continuing reliance on his work.

The nine team roles

Roles	Description and contribution	Allowable weaknesses
Plant	Creative, imaginative, unorthodox. Solves difficult problems.	Ignores details. Too preoccupied to communicate effectively.
Resource investigator	Extrovert, enthusiastic, communicative. Explores opportunities. Develops contacts.	Over-optimistic. Loses interest once initial enthusiasm has passed.
Co-ordinator	Mature, confident, a good chairperson. Clarifies goals, promotes decision making, delegates well.	Can be seen as manipulative. Delegates personal work.
Shaper	Challenging, dynamic, thrives on pressure. Has the drive and courage to overcome obstacles.	Can provoke others. Hurts peoples' feelings.
Monitor–evaluator	Sober, strategic and discerning. Sees all options, judges accurately.	Lacks drive and ability to inspire others. Overly critical.
Teamworker	Co-operative, mild, perceptive and diplomatic. Listens, builds, averts friction, calms the waters.	Indecisive in crunch situations. Can be easily influenced.
Implementer	Disciplined, reliable, conservative and efficient. Turns ideas into practical actions.	Somewhat inflexible. Slow to respond to new responsibilities.
Completer	Painstaking, conscientious, anxious. Searches out errors and omissions. Delivers on time.	Inclined to worry unduly. Reluctant to delegate. Can be a nit picker.
Specialist	Single-minded, self-starting, dedicated. Provides knowledge and skills in rare supply.	Contributes on only a narrow front. Dwells on technicalities. Overlooks the big picture.

If, then, we know that the essential ingredients are embodied in these team roles, and we can test for them, why, you might ask, can we not replicate these success factors and turn out high performing teams like Wolfsburg turns out Volkswagen Golfs?

One answer is that we actually do not know what the team will hit as it progresses along its way. When the team is constituted, we might have a fairly clear idea as to how to bias its capabilities; for example, we might seek to set up a

quality circle type team with a membership strongly representing Teamworker, Implementer, Completer and Specialist
roles. This probably makes sense because of the gradualist
nature of this kind of team. Such a team will produce very
different results if it can draw on Plant, Shaper and Resource
investigator talents as well.

In reality the complexity and dynamism of the system in
which a modern organization operates makes it virtually
impossible to design a team which is both optimal and
durable. Just as a successful individual must be capable of
virtuosity and a wide repertoire of behaviour, so must a high
performing team. Think also for a moment of the most
successful sports team you know, and realize that the
assembled talents which enhance their performance are
diverse and varied.

It is also important when considering team membership
that we do not think of appointing a person to represent each
of the roles outlined by Belbin. This is the kind of resource
to which the manager will rarely have access, especially
when criteria for inclusion must also embrace eligibility
considerations.

My own view is that what each of these roles represents
is a team process. Making sure that these processes are all
occurring in the team is critically important (we return to this
subject later). In practical terms, for team members to
undergo the appropriate psychometric tests makes good
sense. Besides providing useful information to the person
setting up the team, it also starts to raise awareness among
members of team processes.

Shifting membership

The research also shows that few teams have a long-term,
static membership, nor is that much of a surprise given how
frequently things change in the modern organizational
environment. Sometimes, as we saw for example from the
work of Ranney and Deck (6.3) on product development
teams, members are added or shed so that the team's
composition is appropriate to the stage that the developing
product has reached. This is fine so long as the overarch-
ing benefits of cross-functionality are not lost in following this
practice.

Getting new people up to speed within the team is also helped:

■ if the team knows from the outset that its membership will be changing, sometimes by design – a proactive measure, sometimes in response to events – a reactive need;
■ if the team realizes that each member carries a joint responsibility to get new people up and running fast – there is even a case for building this responsibility into the team's operating objectives.

What seems to orientate new members fast and turn them rapidly into valuable contributors is the clarity with which the team is able to describe its mission, vision, values and processes (see later). These are like the rules of the game to a sports team. It is probably possible to learn the rules of football by simply observing play and participating in it but you do learn faster if someone explains them.

Step 6 – Who should lead the team?

We need to draw the distinction between:

■ The manager/sponsor: this is the person who usually sits outside the team. (S)he is usually the person who has assumed responsibility in the organization for the team's success. This is the person who is setting up the team and will be working his/her way through these ten steps.

After the team has been set up, the hands-on aspects of the manager/sponsor's role start to diminish as the team moves through the stages of development.

We have already seen that the manager/sponsor role then changes and needs to concentrate on optimizing the interface between the team and the organization.
■ The team leader: this is the person who sits inside the team and usually starts off as the chairperson managing the briefing, the agendas, the team processes and the internal behavioural development of the team.

This role is obviously very important and starts to become more so as the team goes through the stages of its development – see below and also 'Developing Teams to High Performance' (Chapter 9).

It is very important to be sure that both these roles are filled since there is a great deal of work for each. Often the manager/sponsor is the line manager of the team leader; this is usually the case when a team is an operating unit of an organization.

Where the team is constituted independently of the organization's operating structures or functional departments (a cross-functional quality circle might be an example), the manager/sponsor role might not be as obvious or evident.

Sometimes, the manager/sponsor is also the team leader in which case the person filling that role must be capable of operating in two different spheres and in filling both the specifications below.

The manager/sponsor role

The accountability for the team's success rests, as we have said above, with this person. As such the role consists of:

■ creating the right organizational climate in which the team might flourish – look to Chapter 13, 'Some Important Things to Think About' for some background here;
■ setting up the team and assuring adequate briefing and start-up – the ten-step process is really what this is about;
■ developing the team to high performance – Chapter 9 lays out the responsibilities;
■ acting as facilitator, mentor, counsellor, gopher, ambassador, adviser, resource procurer, feather-smoother, mediator and friend to the team, and for the team to the rest of the organization.

The team leader's role

Among those things that help a team to develop fast is to get clear about what the internal leadership consists of. A useful list might be:

■ Assure that the team is 'on purpose' – doing what it is supposed to be doing.
■ Assure the allocation of work and resources within the team.

High Performing Teams

- Assure that the team processes take place (as already mentioned, we will come to a more detailed description of the processes later, but for the moment let us assume that they equate to the team roles outlined above).
- Assure that the information flow between the team and the manager/sponsor is working well – this can sometimes mean keeping the manager/sponsor's anxiety levels within bounds.
- Assure that the team balances its time between achieving its objectives and monitoring its effectiveness (more of this, some of it woo woo, when we get to feedback, below).

Options for team leadership

- Appoint a leader – selecting from the candidate members the most appropriate person. This is the most usual course.
- Rotate the leadership among members – rules must be established; how long, in what order will rotation occur etc. Sometimes this is an option exercised later in the team's development. It is sometimes used when an existing leader role is vacated. One of its great benefits is the personal development and experience it can build for the individual in (if the team is working well) a relatively low risk environment.
- Have the team elect a leader – establish conditions, e.g. leaders must be permanent not transitory members; fix a time period which may be renewable.
- Consider a self-directed team – i.e. given its operating brief and those elements of the objectives which will get it going, ask it to determine the approach it will take to leadership. This must allow for it not to appoint a leader but rather to organize itself on an intrafunctional basis. There are successful precedents – see the Public Service case report in Chapter 6.

Just as it is hard to predict the bias we should give to team roles when we set the team up, so it is hard to define those that which make for a successful leader. Belbin, in his extensive research, found that not even above-average mental ability adequately predicted success. He did find though that if the leader could not keep up with the team this predisposed both leader and team to failure.

Versatility of behaviour, excellence in communication, good analytical reasoning and thinking ability; those things that generally make for successful leadership equally make for successful team leadership.

Step 7 – What rules need to be established?

A distinguishing characteristic of high performing teams, as we keep saying, is their clarity of purpose. Teams need to know why they are there. The requirement is broader than agreeing objectives; they need to know the context in which they are expected to operate and the strategic or tactical purpose they are expected to fulfil. Even teams with a limited life expectancy like some task force teams or project teams need to understand purpose clearly. Without this contextual background it is often hard to develop the objectives necessary to drive the team activity forward.

Mission and purpose

The systemic type of team, one that is going to be part of the organization's systems for a while, will need to spend some time developing a mission. Mission statements are much derided because they usually suffer from the twin disabilities of sounding lumpen and trite, but it is the process of developing a mission or purpose statement rather than the statement itself that will supply some of the glue the team will need to bind it together.

Mission or purpose, if it is to serve the team, must also have a discernible lineal descent through the organization. In other words, the team's mission or purpose statement must be a subset of the organization's overall mission and declared purpose. As organizations get flatter and there are fewer obfuscatory layers between the top and the bottom, the interlocking nature of the mission or purpose statements, each a subset of another, starts to provides critical orientation for the team and for each individual who serves on it.

An analogy which has contributed greatly to understanding the power of mission is that of George Ainsworth-Land (8.1), general systems scientist and savant. Mission is likened to DNA in the biological cell. Every cell within an organism will contain the DNA which defines the function of that cell and the nature of the organism of which it is a part. A human body is composed of so many cells that it is an inherently unmanageable system; the only principle on which it can be organized is if every single cell is quite clear, because of its DNA, as to its micro and macro purpose.

Mission then is the DNA of the organization. If the team is to discharge both its micro and macro purpose it must be aligned with the overall organizational purpose as well as be clear about its specific contribution.

Vision

Clarity about mission can be productively enhanced by getting some clarity too about vision – what success looks (and maybe even feels) like when the team achieves it. Spending some time on this will also help the team bridge more easily into agreeing team objectives.

Values

A final steering mechanism for the team is the concept of values. Increasingly organizations are expected to be able to predicate the values by which they attempt to operate. Well beyond the limitations imposed by compliance are the ethical and environmental considerations which are increasingly driving investors and are usually important to employees.

Again, time is usually productively spent in agreeing the team's values. These really fall into two clear categories of consideration. The first requires examining the implication of the organization's declared values on the team's functions and activities and deciding how the team will mirror them and sustain their integrity.

The second group of values has to do with the team deciding how it wishes to conduct its activity. In dealing with this it helps to draw attention to the fact that the team is about to enter the woo woo realm; it also helps to make it clear that the evidence is that doing so is a precondition of their becoming a high performing team.

Some of the values which high performing teams will set for themselves are:

■ being open to difference – recognizing that the view of others may differ from your own, but allowing the integrity of that view;
■ telling the truth – surfacing differences for discussion, and, if possible, resolution;
■ dealing with mutual irritation – being prepared to declare and seek agreement to mutual changes in behaviour about things that irritate or annoy;
■ being reliable – doing the things you undertake to do for the team;
■ being considerate – showing up on time for meetings, accepting a modicum of inconvenience to discharge your team responsibilities;
■ being bound by team decisions – differ by all means but do not undermine a decision to which the team has committed.

Developing a list of values starts the woo woo juices flowing and also starts to provide the team with a basis of self and mutual evaluation. Besides being a critical differentiator of the high performing team, agreement about values anticipates some of the problems the team and its leader will need to solve when it moves into the storming stage of its development.

Step 8 – What sort of objectives will be needed?

One of the first tangible outputs of a newly constituted team should be a list of the objectives it intends to achieve. Most teams will not have a great deal of difficulty in defining objectives, especially if the briefing which has gone before has met the criteria of context and purpose which are so important to establish.

Team objectives, if we are aspiring to high performance, should differ from those which an individual might agree with his/her manager in some respects. To assure that the team hits the ground running, three characteristics should be present.

■ Objectives should conform to the usual SMART criteria. They should also show an appropriate level of integration into the organizational context that spawned the team.

- The definition of objectives must address itself to the question of how the team will know that it has achieved what it has set out to achieve. This may sound mind-numbingly obvious, but in the systemic team, one that will be around for some time, it may be necessary to create a means of measurement which does not currently exist. This has proved especially true with quality circle type teams. Their objective plainly is to improve quality, but we need to have indices of what we are achieving now, so that we will know we are improving.

- The last attribute, and the one that distinguishes high performing team goals from conventional objective setting activities, has to do with the team undertaking to review and monitor its own performance against its purpose and values, its processes and its objectives.

Step 9 – What feedback loops will have to be in place?

It is a personal belief, but one that I believe is shared among people involved in team development, that the way in which a team monitors itself is one of the unproven differentiators of the high performing team.

Called by its more familiar name, 'feedback' is, as they say, 'the breakfast of champions'. Performance improvement depends to a huge extent on access to, and the quality of, feedback provided. There are only two types of feedback:

- reinforcing feedback – designed to identify and get agreement around the elements or component parts of achieved success, and then consolidating those elements into ongoing activity;

- change-directed feedback – designed to identify and gain agreement around the elements or component parts of a perceived failure or shortfall in performance, agreeing how these elements might be changed or eliminated and consolidating the changes into ongoing activity.

Negative feedback is not really feedback, it is just criticism. If things are not working as we want them, the issue is to understand why, and what it is we need to change in order to achieve our intention. It is that change which needs to be incorporated into activity.

The high performing team needs to be able to generate its own feedback because much of what it needs to get feedback about, its processes for example, is known only to the team members in their interactions with each other. It is for this reason that the team must incorporate regular feedback or self-monitoring activities into its objectives.

In Hilarie Owen's Creating Top Flight Teams (8.2) she shares with us her experience in working with the Red Arrows – the Royal Air Force's famous aerial acrobatic team. By any criteria this is a high performing team, and Ms Owen tells us much of how they achieve it. Among the most compelling aspects, though, is the fact that every rehearsal and every performance of the Red Arrows is videoed, and every video is viewed and critiqued by all members in the team. As cogent a piece of feedback as one could imagine and, I would guess, a critical adjunct to improvement and (see later) to team learning.

There are three critical feedback loops for which the team must legislate:

■ how it is doing against purpose and values;
■ how it is doing against team processes;
■ how it is doing against agreed objectives.

Each of these aspects deserves consideration.

Feedback against purpose and values

Just as in life we frequently lose sight of purpose in a welter of busyness, so the team is likely to deviate or lose its way as events, successes and failures influence what it does. Asking the critical question 'Are we doing what we were set up to do?' helps re-establish the validity of objectives, priorities and, if necessary, the need to change.

Furthermore, if the team has spent the time, as it should have, in declaring the values by which it is going to operate, it must pause now and then to consider whether it is meeting its own criteria. Examining its conformity to its own values-based specifications will lead the team either to revise its specification or to develop a series of contracts to improve and enhance aspects of individual performance which are not meeting criteria.

High Performing Teams

Dealing with these kinds of issues is part of the process of improving team performance. It is not self-indulgent, and though it takes time, high performing teams find it an activity which is imperative to sustain their success.

Feedback against team process criteria

Undertaking a process review requires that the team looks carefully at how it is doing against those processes that we know characterize successful teams. One of the ways teams do this is by extending and adapting Belbin's Team Roles into a process catechism as follows:

■ In our team activities are we:
  producing imaginative and creative solutions?
  exploring opportunities and developing external contacts?
  clarifying and promoting decision taking and delegating appropriately?
  sufficiently challenging and sufficiently resolved to overcome obstacles?
  looking at all options and judging well?
  listening to each other and dealing with interpersonal friction?
  producing the means for practical implementation?
  careful to look for errors and omissions?
  accessing sufficient specialist skills?

In the above, the Team Role name has been eliminated and the description of the contribution has been reframed as a question.

It is a useful tool and in my experience generates a level of discussion and self-examination for the team to be able to focus on how it might improve its processes, or possibly even reassure itself that it is doing the right things.

Feedback against objectives

The team must take time out to monitor how it is doing against its objectives. We have already spelt out the need for creating explicit measures which indicate that we have achieved, or are on the way to achieving, agreed objectives. If objectives are there to help 'pull' the team, as they should, then the team needs to be reminded of them regularly and take the time to consider seriously how they are progressing. Using milestones, defined events indicating forward progress, is one of the techniques teams use.

A subject we have touched on already, and will return to later, is that of the 'learning organization'. This is an organizational construct which many, including the author, believe provides a viable and essential model for the future. The provision of feedback loops, the insistence on the team critiquing their own performance, the team's positive attitude and preparedness to engage in feedback are all essential disciplines, the practice of which starts to help build a learning organization.

Step 10 – What training will the team need?

In planning for the training and development of the team we need to consider two different levels.

Functional training

For the individual team member we need to be sure that what is asked of that person is within his/her ability to provide. Membership of a team often draws people into unfamiliar territory or requires of them skills and disciplines which they may have not previously encountered. Individually tailored training programmes, addressed at developing the necessary business or functional skills needs, must be planned for and implemented. In this respect one might be talking of skills like Project Management, Budgeting, Planning etc.

Sometimes this requirement may be met by the appraisal and staff development systems that the organization operates outside the team environment. In the UK where the Investors in People initiative is becoming more broadly implemented in organizations, it is increasingly likely that employees are involved, usually with their line managers, in a regular assessment of their training requirements. Assuring that the line manager is sensitive to the potential demands for functional training that team membership may be creating in the employee is an important piece of co-ordination to get right.

Team development training

Collective team training is the other level of productive involvement. High performing teams tend to know quite a lot about the dynamics of teams. They may have learnt this from observing their own activity, but to accelerate the process, most successful teams tend to benefit from a sustained team development programme. This can usefully be built around workshops integrating development with the real business of the team.

Effective workshops can accelerate the process of establishing purpose statements, mission and shared vision. They can also speed up objective setting and the identification of priorities for the team. In Chapter 13 of this book we lay out a model which relates training needs to the phases of team development. This model goes into greater depth describing the nature of the training which might be provided at each stage.

There is value too in developing interpersonal skills in team members to help provide the ground rules for dealing with differences. Katzenbach and Smith (6.9) clearly differentiate the need for interpersonal training from team development training. I remain unconvinced of the effectiveness of separating them. Developing and practising interpersonal skills with the colleagues with whom it is critical you use them seems to provide a symmetrical development which accelerates understanding and reinforces usage.

Using the numerous psychometric instruments available also helps members build an understanding of team dynamics and the behaviour which is most productive in sustaining it.

A good ground rule is that the team should meet twice a year to focus intensively on the process of enhancing their effectiveness as a team. Differentiating between the business agenda and the development agenda helps position the importance of the latter. Subsequently re-integrating the interpersonal and business strands within the workshop seems to add relevance to members. These sessions are usually better placed under the care of a facilitator who also helps by example to refresh the normal processes of the team's meetings.

Executive summary

ACTION

Ten questions to have answered before setting up a team

1. What's the issue that needs solution?

Get clear about the underlying issue – cure, not symptom reduction

Realize being able to make a clear statement of purpose is critical

2. Is a team the best solution?

Against – slow to gel, will take management time, risk of failure

For – advantages of cross-functionality, buy-in and commitment, develop people, change the game, access creativity

3. What sort of team?

Options: task force, quality circle type, project team

Considerations: problem solving charter or systemic team

4. What will it take to sustain the team in the organization?

Defence – how will I protect and defend it?

Change – can I change the way I do things?

5. Who should be on the team?

Eligible – the best qualified

Suitable – people likely to make the most useful contribution

6. Who should lead the team ?

Establish – leader, leadership rules

Define – leader role

7. What rules need to be established?

You will need . . .   in order to establish. . .

Mission

Vision   Objectives

Values

8. What sort of objectives will be needed?

SMART

How will we know we're getting there?

Become self-monitoring

9. What feedback loops will have to be in place?

Loop 1 – Purpose, vision and values

Loop 2 – Team processes

Loop 3 – Objectives

10. What training will the team need?

Functional – business skills training for each individual

Team Development – collectively for the team

9 Developing teams to high performance

This chapter starts from having set up the team and leads the manager through the stages the team will encounter as it develops. It describes what is happening at each stage within the team, provides advice on how to manage it. It also makes suggestions on sustaining high performance.

Taking time to develop

Most researchers, practitioners and commentators agree that teams take time to develop. If a work group, say an existing department within an organization, is charged with the responsibility of becoming a team, there will at least be a familiarity among members, and probably some experience of each others' work activities and practices. It may seem reasonable to expect that this familiarity would speed up the time taken for the group to come together as a team. This is not the case, however, and often it takes longer than putting together a cross-functional team where there is little previous experience of the work required or of others in the team.

Turning existing work groups into teams poses the central question of what will be different as a result of being called a team, rather than, say, the Bought Ledger Department. Explanations, which inevitably centre on the way in which the work will be done, will be greeted with incredulity, disbelief and usually cynicism. Most people believe they are already working hard and doing a good job, and they find it difficult to take the leap of the imagination necessary to mobilize their commitment to change things on what look like slender grounds. The benefits anticipated, because they inevitably rest on improved productivity and enhanced overall performance, will usually be seen, at best, as illusory and, at worst, as insulting.

When Caterpillar in Peoria moved existing service departments to team-based operations (see Chapter 5), it did so in an environment where the whole business was reorganizing itself and moving to individual profit and service centres. A climate of organizational change coincided with an increase in the expectations of internal customers of the levels of service they were currently receiving. If this was the carrot, the stick too was being wielded because it was made clear that if internal departments were incapable of achieving standards of service provided by outside suppliers, then it was the outside suppliers who would get the business.

Commitment gathered momentum only after a number of visits to other companies had been undertaken and other successful applications had been investigated. Even after six months of operating as a team, the first pilot volunteer work group was still questioning whether they should continue the experiment.

There is evidence that it is easier to kick off a new, cross-functional team of people who may not previously have worked closely together. Provided with clear purpose, at least the reasons for their existence are more comprehensible, and the expectation of success more easily understood.

What takes time with new teams, where members are less familiar with each other, is just that: the unfamiliarity. Energy is spent on assessing others, establishing personal positions, looking for allies and creating relationships. The focus on purpose and objectives, the business of the team, is likely to lag well behind these necessary preliminaries.

The issue that confronts managers is how to accelerate the development processes of any new team so that it moves to higher levels of performance as quickly as possible.

There is general agreement that teams go through stages of development. The most commonly accepted approach, as much for the insights it offers as because it sounds so memorable, is Tuckman's four-stage forming, storming, norming and performing development process.

High Performing Teams

To speed up team development each of these stages can be effectively managed, sometimes by the manager/sponsor but more usually by the team leader. Being aware of what the team is likely to go through at each of these stages allows the team leader to plan for ways of navigating through them. It also helps the team deal with what is going on in team meetings when the behaviour of members can be, at least partially, explained by placing it in a developmental context.

As with all protracted undertakings, the better the planning, the higher the chances of success. Much of the detail outlined in the Ten Steps in the last chapter is designed to help accelerate the process. It does this by building a really robust framework in which the team can operate. By agreeing the rules, and all the rules (mission, vision, values, processes, objectives and feedback loops) in advance, the team does not have to stop and invent them as they go along. It is usually tough enough to keep up with the business of the day without having to take time out to construct context.

Another useful, if less memorable, model for team development is the three-phase process conforming by and large to the 'S' or growth curve. In this format we have a development process which looks like this:

Group of individuals
↓
Team
↓
High performing team or
Self-directed team

It is part of the philosophy of the growth curve that the 'final' stage, usually called the integrative stage because it integrates all the lessons of the past into a new approach to the future, is, in fact, never final. Rather it helps to provide the lessons by which continuous and constant renewal must take place.

This ongoing need for renewal fits well with most people's experience of high performing teams. Even the best teams are likely to get stuck, run out of steam, need help or some kind of renewal. We need to provide for this eventuality, or more properly, this inevitability.

Again, Tuckman's four-stage forming, storming, norming, performing approach helps restart stalled teams. Sometimes stuck teams have reverted to an earlier stage of development and if they can perceive this themselves, they can also find their way out again. Sometimes it just needs somebody to tell them where they are to get them going again.

In dealing with the processes of accelerating a team to high performance we will follow a blend of approaches:

- Forming – the behaviour of a group of individuals
- Storming and norming – the emergence of team behaviour
- Performing and reforming – maintaining and renewing high performance

In each of these sections we will also look at the leadership task needed to accelerate development, and offer some processes which have been successful in other applications.

The development process

Forming – a group of individuals

In most applications, a group of people will have been identified as a future team, a purpose or set of objectives will have been determined, and the leader will have outlined some sort of vision, belief or set of expectations about what will be achieved by the teaming process.

Members will not necessarily have been part of formulating this opening brief; indeed they rarely are. They will not necessarily 'buy' any part of this bill of goods and will probably be sceptical if not overtly hostile. Some may not wish to be there at all, and most will be suspicious that the process will probably use more of their time, cause them to work harder or deflect their efforts from their 'real work'. More positively, most people react well to the idea of being part of a team with the sense of belonging and sharing problems and successes. Emotions, then, are likely to be mixed.

The leadership role is plainly to create a compelling and attractive view of what might be achieved. The aim has to be to bring the members of the team on board, to get their buy-in, to generate some enthusiasm; at least to encourage members to put their disbelief on hold. Essentially the leader must deal with both the personal reward and the potential business pay-off, not only of success but also of participation.

When the individuals in the group (because we are still far from being a team) are prepared to accept the basic charter and the leader's vision of what might be achieved, behaviour in the group will change. Each individual becomes engaged in asserting a personal role as well as judging the roles and characteristics of others in the group. Members are usually polite and considerate of others. Views expressed will be tentative or at least guarded. Criticism and detracting comment will be directed against the organization rather than the leader or each other.

Strong and probably lasting impressions will be formed of each other and this will start to mark out the potential alliances of the future. Lots of 'what if', scenario-type questions will be put and the probable corporate consequences of success and failure will be tested. Little will be committed and most members will describe themselves as keeping their options open.

Purpose will be tested again and again and what will start to emerge is the need to make some definitions of the power of the team. What happens to team decisions? Will they go elsewhere for ratification and action? Will the team have the right to implement? What are the interfaces with existing decision-making mechanisms within the organization, and how will difference or conflict with these existing systems be resolved?

Early processes should devote time to establishing clarity around purpose, and to gaining the first cut at objectives and the milestones by which the team will be able to gauge its progress towards achieving them. Getting clear about the positioning of the team within the organization hierarchy will help members relate their efforts to corporate intention too.

Leaders find the need to implicate the group – get their fingerprints on the purpose and on the objectives. While members are unlikely to reach true consensus, we can at least aim for participation in establishing a longer-term vision and a shorter-term set of priorities. In part we are looking for the group to endorse the intention in setting them up, but we are also looking for them to refine and start to elaborate and develop that intention.

To do this, breakouts of smaller groups help to force serious consideration and thoughtful feedback. Often a facilitator can contribute a lot to getting the group up and running at this early stage. The time taken to reach agreement can be telescoped down and the presence of an honest broker tends to deflect potential suspicion of the leadership's motives.

Experience has shown that if the leader establishes a strong agenda in these early stages, thus indicating an expectation of busyness and activity for the team, some of the unresolved issues may simply evaporate, at least temporarily.

Forming can sometimes expose really deep divisions in the priorities of members and this will need to be resolved before the team can start to deal with the real work. Sometimes these differences can be anticipated, often they come as a surprise to all members of the team.

The author facilitated a forming meeting of the most senior management of a motor car distributor with a number of sales outlets throughout the UK. The intention was to form a new top team approach, integrating a board which had grown rather remote from operations with the most senior line of operational management.

Initial passes were made at developing an overall purpose statement which would guide the team's activities, and it rapidly became clear that two quite separate agendas were at work. The board saw the key issue the team should address as enhancing the profitability of the company and hence its ability to satisfy the shareholders with improved dividends. The operational management saw the team's major purpose as improving levels of customer satisfaction both in its sales and in its vehicle servicing activities.

On the face of it, these views are easily reconcilable. The board's view represented the 'what', the operational management's view represented the 'how'. A next level of exploration exposed an even deeper difference. The board saw a future strategy which looked to margin improvement and cost reduction, whereas the operational management saw a strategy based on growing market share.

It became the team's first order of business to build a viable medium-term strategy which balanced the competing views. The original intention of a better integrated top team was achieved almost covertly because a focus (purpose) in which all members of the team felt the deepest involvement emerged.

There is no specified length of time for the forming phase of a team. Nor is it possible to define an exact moment at which the team moves from forming to storming. Both processes take place side by side because while one of the conditions for ending the forming phase is agreement on purpose, another is the building of relationships.

In the case of the motor car distributor above, the initial forming meeting was quite successful in establishing purpose. On the other hand it set back the interpersonal relationship aspects because each of the factions within the top team were now much more wary of the intentions of the other. This leads us to . . .

Storming . . .

Storming is inevitably a period of conflict. Even in the most ordered and polite societies or corporate environments a team will go through a process of storming. Individual members, or the sub-groups and alliances which have formed, compete, test each other, test the leadership, challenge the ground rules, attack the corporate environment, reject the purpose and so on. The energy of the team is being directed not at achieving the purpose or the objectives but in two other directions:

■ questioning and attacking the constitutional framework in which the team is operating;
■ challenging each other, sub-groups within the team, and most especially challenging the leader.

The best one can hope for during the storming phase is that it does not take too long, since little is accomplished while it is happening. The other hope is that it does not spill out of the team environment and start to poison the organizational culture.

Storming is the period when the role of the team leader is probably at its most important. Essentially this consists of:

- allowing a forum for the moaning and groaning;
- setting strong ground rules which prohibit attacks on individuals but allow facts to be challenged – hard on the issues, but soft on the people;
- renegotiating those ground rules (usually corporate) which are clearly limiting the team's effectiveness;
- re-asserting the processes which help the team, re-asserting the vision, re-asserting the values;
- identifying and supporting visible strengths within the team;
- resolving conflict and limiting the damage of confrontation;
- boosting morale and remaining confident;
- above all, remaining cool and being able to cope with the attacks which will inevitably be made on the leader.

What is happening within the storming process is, at one level, power plays, and at another people are dealing with the personal threats and readjustments which may be starting to emerge because the team is embracing functions of which the individual has previously held custody. People are protecting their turf.

Usually the team is raising fundamental or strategic questions for the organization which might be seen as threatening to individuals or sub-groups. Alternatively members may see great opportunities emerging for themselves or the factions they represent. Storming fuels the exercise of corporate politics and it will continue until the energy it uses can be channelled into the more productive courses of the purpose and objectives of the team.

During the storming process, team morale and individual confidence diminish. It looks as if the team will never be able to do what is intended. People feel stressed and unhappy. It is at this point that teams are most likely to fail and throw in the towel. The ability of the team leader to hang on, believe in a new dawn, and get others to believe that too, is critical.

Perhaps of even more danger to the organization is the 'team' which finds storming a convenient forum in which to continue to participate without any intention of ever developing beyond. There is evidence that many organizations continue to harbour storming 'teams' which are not only grounded on the reefs of mutual suspicion and recrimination but also happy to be there. Biased and partial information is disclosed at meetings, positions are taken, action is proposed and never implemented. The lesson is that if you have one of these 'teams', move it on or throttle it off.

... and norming – the emergence of team behaviour

Norming starts to emerge when the conflicts which the group has raised in the storming process are either resolved or, more often, accepted. Personal defensiveness is replaced by unemotional statements of concern and sometimes even requests for help. Attacks are replaced by content-rich, emotion-free feedback. Rules of conduct and process are followed rather than having to be continuously asserted by the leader.

Mutual support, collective and team responsibility start to emerge. Information is used to illuminate rather than, as in the storming process, to exercise power. Relationships deepen, members make allowances for each other, and individuals are prepared to take greater personal risk.

It is here that we start to see what is intended by accelerating the development cycle of the team by embedding some of the processes of norming into the eye of the storming. It rests in having established with the team a set of rules of conduct which, at the time they were agreed, were probably seen as being irrelevant or at least over-elaborate in their provision. These are the rules alluded to in the Executive summary in Chapter 8. They embrace the following:

- team values;
- team processes;
- providing feedback loops to assure the team was evaluating its performance against these criteria.

Having an agreed charter of this kind to hand helps the leader orientate the group and deal more productively with the dysfunctionality that happens during storming. By the time norming emerges, the leader's role starts to be less interventionist and more about assuring that the team conforms to its mission, vision, values and objectives. It is about creating more time for the woo woo because a team in the norming phase starts to understand the strength the woo woo will bring them.

It is fair to say that teams which have won through to the norming stage are still not entirely focused on their purpose and objectives. Energy is still being siphoned off and applied to the norming process. Thought and effort is being spent on how best to work together and on being careful and helpful. The team will not yet have reached the stage when all this is automatic and unconscious. When the team achieves this, it will have entered its most productive stage, described as . . .

Performing

When you are here, you have reached the goal. You will know it by the quality and completeness of the work which the team is regularly achieving, and by the speed with which it is doing so. High performance output rarely merely meets criteria, it usually exceeds it, 'delighting the customer' as our Caterpillar teams put it.

Among the things that start to assert themselves is the breadth and comprehensiveness of the team's activity. It rarely misses tricks, fails to think things through, or neglects to anticipate. The benefit of several brains – all focused and all energized – achieves this. It rarely fails to meet its deadlines and never falls short of the commitments it sets itself.

Work is switched among members and apportioned by the team with fairness, and also with a recognition of the most appropriate person to deal with it. The team examines the upsides and downsides of situations and assumes account-ability when it decides to take risks.

The team's flow of energy is focused entirely on purpose and objectives. Perhaps this is why so much is achieved; little of the effort is seeping away into:

- establishing relationships, because they are established;
- minimizing personal risk, because the team will jointly support the risk;
- establishing personal position, because that is under-stood by colleagues;

High Performing Teams

- defence, because members are not under attack from each other;
- winkling out information, because information (and opinion) is freely exchanged.

Members of the team are exhilarated by their success and they derive more reward and satisfaction from their work. They become confident and assured – they're on a roll, they are a high performing team. Personal behaviour of members not only demonstrates high levels of trust, but also the ability to anticipate the views and needs of others within the group. Differences are surfaced and resolved, feedback is volunteered and, when given, it is accepted. The team has fun, enjoys meeting, it assigns mock stereotypes to each other and everyone lives up to the stereotype that has been assigned to him or her.

The above does not imply that no disagreement occurs, nor that the team is undivided in its views or in its priorities. It simply means that it has the means of achieving resolution without heads being broken. Phenomenal leaps in productivity result, breakthroughs occur and log jams are demolished.

The internal leadership of the team usually becomes less assertive, and indeed where the leadership resides may not be clear at all. The team will have become so competent at chairing itself and allocating work and resources that it hardly needs a leader to legitimize its decisions. Members of the team will also anticipate the team's role or potential role in developments which occur outside it, in the organization or in the customer bases it serves. Rather than the leader needing to introduce an agenda to the team, each member will be bringing a relevant agenda.

The leader's task is to remain vigilant for any signs of emerging dysfunctionality within the team, between the team and its sponsor/manager, and between the team and the organization. Successful teams are often more vulnerable to attacks from the oft mentioned organization immune system than relative low performing or semi-dormant teams. The reason is obvious: organizations are always alert to shifts of power and have a natural bias towards restoring homeostasis.

The task of external management of the team, usually the role of the manager/sponsor, changes entirely and much more time must be spent representing the cause and the decisions of the team to the organization at large. Resources must be won for the team, sponsorship expanded and a sound internal public relations job must be done in part to maximixe the team's effectiveness within the organization, in part to let it know that the organization recognizes performance, places value on it, and seeks to reward it.

Above all, the manager/sponsor and all the members of the team should enjoy, relish, delight in and celebrate this performing stage. Doing so reinforces it, causes the team to examine why it is successful and to replicate the processes that lie behind its success.

Performing . . . maintaining and renewing

High performing teams generate great momentum of their own. This happens, as we have seen, because members are sustained by the reward of their palpable success, by the relationships they have established with others in the team and by their general sense of job satisfaction.

But nothing, as the sage says, fails as certainly as success. There are things that happen inside the team which cause it to falter, and there are obviously things that happen outside it which may affect it negatively. Changes of strategy, changes of management, internal reorganizations – all those things to which every organization is prone will obviously affect the team. Sometimes the need for the team is vitiated, sometimes the purpose is so radically changed that we have the wrong team. The game changes as certainly for teams as it does for the organizations for which they work. It is for these reasons that at the front end of the whole process of setting up teams clarity of intention or purpose is critical. In Chapter 13 this is put as a simple question: 'If you have got it (a team) can you use it?'

Internally, teams do run out of steam; or they feel that they have no more Everests to climb, they may see their original purpose as being fulfilled. The challenge of continual improvement may be insufficiently exhilarating: 'did we go through all that storming to so little purpose?'. Often this disillusion is a function of the reward or recognition which the team is achieving. Sometimes it may be disappointment at the potential scope of its future activity.

Preventing the internal collapse, or dealing with the internal despondency which a team may feel as the result of major corporate change, relies on getting re-aligned again. Robbins and Finley in Why Teams Don't Work (2.1) describe it as a continuous process of clarifying the clarity. This means that the team constantly needs to revisit its basics and align themselves with them.

What are those basics? Overwhelmingly they remain the Purpose/Mission, Vision, and Values. If they have changed, and they might have, it is critically important for the team to realize this and to get comfortable with the change if they can. Often teams see themselves as having been diverted, deflected, subtly redirected from their original understandings. If this sort of manipulation is suspected then it needs to be confronted rather than concealed. Confrontation of the fact alone often unsticks a stuck team.

The other key basic is the integrity with which the team is adhering to its agreed processes. One of the feedback loops we advocated in Step 9 of setting up teams was finding a way for the team to judge how it is performing against its agreements about processes. Perceiving drift against these criteria may help a team right itself with a new set of resolutions and refreshed intention.

If we are looking at having to do a substantial renewal of the team, the growth curve school of development has most to offer us. The growth curve anticipates a decline in performance and seeks to renew by integrating the best of the past with the new direction of the future.

The best things of the past are those that have achieved success once, and the question might for example be how to carry forward the values, maybe some of the vision too, and re-assemble these around a new purpose. The other relevant aspect of the past which can be integrated is the insistence on monitoring performance against team processes.

Each of the shifts and renewals the team has to accommodate will have its parallels within the forming, storming, norming and performing developmental process the team has already undergone. Some of the behaviour which was evident in those stages will re-emerge, and the leadership task is to manage it as adroitly, if not more adroitly, the second, third or 'n'th time around. It helps, of course, that the team will be largely familiar with the replay in which it is engaged, and members will also have more confidence that they will re-emerge from their dysfunctionality as they have done in the past. The whole pace then should be faster.

High performing teams, like high performing cars, need constant maintenance. Neglect does not mean that they function less efficiently, but that they do not function at all, or that they become dangerous and potentially destructive.

Executive summary

Stage of development	Team behaviour	Leadership role – to accelerate development
Forming – group of individuals	• Each asserts a personal role • Alliances are sought and formed • Judgements made of each other • Polite co-operative atmosphere	• Keep asserting the purpose • Allow time and opportunity for relationships to form • Develop team support of vision, values and processes
Storming	• Attack the constitution and framework in which the team must operate • Attack the leader • Challenge each other – power plays • Defend own turf • Low morale and confidence	• Keep asserting purpose, vision, values and processes • Renegotiate ground rules within the team or outside within organization • Limit/prohibit personal attacks • Resolve conflict • Keep cheerful and confident
Norming – emergence of team behaviour	• Acceptance of ground rules • Information starts to be shared • Start of focus on purpose and objectives • Mutual support starts to emerge	• Keep focus on objectives and help prioritize • Chairperson-type behaviour • Provide feedback personally and activate the feedback loops • Represent the team to the organization
Performing – the high performing team	• High degree of focus on purpose and objectives • Rapid and appropriate assignment of tasks • Output exceeds expectations in quality and speed	• Provide feedback personally and activate the feedback loops • Represent the team to the organization • Provide PR for the team • Provide rewards for team performance
Maintaining – renewing and integrating	• Team loses heart – runs out of steam, becomes disillusioned	• Integrate values, feedback and positives of the past into present • Provide stretch goals • Revert to appropriate development phase

10 Teams and contemporary management trends

This chapter takes a brief look at the environment in which modern management operates. It then considers eight key management ideas, trends or initiatives of importance to modern managers, relates what each is, how it works and the role and contribution of teams to it.

The changing business environment

Because this chapter will look at the relationship between teams and some of the newer management ideas, initiatives and trends it will, inevitably, revisit some of the ideas we discussed earlier in the book on extending the teaming concept.

First, where do all these new ideas come from? The management press expands prodigiously with scores of important journals and a rich annual output of books. New ideas are constantly arising, case studies of success and failure are reported (although those documenting failure are pretty rare). Some of the ideas that arise are mere fads, some are important breakthroughs. Below we look at a selection of those ideas; as far as possible I hope to have identified and discarded the fads and concentrated on those movements which are likely to be more durable. I have, for example, omitted comment on the recent Fortune article which appears to imply that managers innovate more successfully when immersed naked, with their mentors, in hot tubs!

The environment in which organizations are operating

Teaming, we have established, is a means of enhancing performance by unlocking synergy. It should be seen as an enabler to achieving business objectives, rather than an objective in itself. Nonetheless much of contemporary management thinking rests upon the potential advantages of high performing teams to underpin the effective implementation of change.

We have already spoken about the shifting environment in which most companies operate. Essentially the pace of change is accelerating and hence companies must re-invent themselves more frequently. Things are unlikely to slow down, and the future is unlikely to become more predictable. While this is true of the competitive environment in which companies operate, the world of work is, of course, far larger than the company environment alone. Not-for-profit organizations, government, education etc. all represent substantial numbers of employed people; in some countries the public sector employs larger numbers than does the private sector.

It is fair to say that the ways in which the public sector and the private sector are managed are becoming increasingly similar. Within the UK, especially in the Thatcher years, the policy of privatization flourished. The policy has been widely adopted in other countries as well. Deregulation of actual or de facto monopolies has occurred in a number of major industries; utilities and telecommunications in particular have been affected.

Market testing, the practice of seeking outside providers of services which have previously been performed within vertically integrated organizations, has also flourished. Many operational aspects of government in Britain have been converted from departments within ministries to independently managed agencies. The status of substantial parts of the health service and the educational establishment has been redefined to instil a greater degree of competitiveness, more autonomy and self-determination and lower cost operation. Britain is not alone in this experience; most of Europe is moving in the same direction too.

Within the past few years we have also seen the collapse of the communist economic structure, and one of the effects of this is to propel from state control into private operation and ownership not just pieces of industries, but huge tranches of whole national economies.

Without the traditional divides of private and public sector, and capitalist and communist economies, organizations are confronting fairly similar problems and hence behaving in very similar ways across the whole world. Of course one cannot ignore national differences which greatly affect the climate and conduct of organizations in different countries, but there is probably more similarity in international management behaviour, public and private sector, at the end of the twentieth century than there has been since the days when most of the world was run by a few colonial giants.

The effect of this is, as we have seen, that the smorgasbord of management initiatives has more dishes on it than ever before. Moreover, most organizations are dining from the same table whereas formerly the public and private sectors, the communist and the capitalist worlds, might even have been using different dining rooms. The problem for the manager is to select which of the dishes from the rich smorgasbord of options represents the most nourishing meal for the organization.

It is probably fair to say that of the newer management initiatives which people might either be merely flirting with, or perhaps trying out now, some will become core to organizational thinking and operations in the future as we have seen happen in the past.

An example we are all familiar with is Japanese quality circles. The thinking behind them, if not the specific technique, has been transplanted, with cultural adaptation, across the world. In our roles as consumers, we would have to acknowledge that the quality of almost anything we now buy or use is better than it was two decades ago. Whether quality circles have driven these improvements or not is less of an issue than the fact that the competitive environment has asserted the primacy of fitness for purpose. Quality installed as a managerial commitment is probably more important than the technique of the quality circle. What we have seen, and what we reap the benefit of as consumers, is that while quality circles might have been dismissable as a trendy fad of a couple of decades ago, they have in essence transformed the way companies operate and the way customers' needs are met.

The other scenario is that ripples of enthusiasm are generated about a new management idea or technique. The gurus usually pronounce positively rather than endorsing with fervour or dismissing it out of hand (who knows, it might just take off). Three or four definitive books emerge and reputations and fortunes are made. The consulting companies bolt a new vocabulary onto the front end of their traditional analytical work study approach and, lo!, a new consulting product is born.

It takes time, however, either to prove the uselessness of the concept, which is very rare (almost any new approach will have some, at least Hawthorn effect, pay-off) or to refine it so that it really starts to help in the management of the organization. It also seems that this utility only starts to emerge when the senior management of organizations start to believe it will work and lend the support of their commitment.

Business process re-engineering

Davenport, Hammer and Champny's business process re-engineering is a good example of a current debate raging away. Whether it is a vogue or not remains to be seen. The technique has the highest profile, with Time magazine recently selecting Hammer as one of the 25 most influential Americans.

Process re-engineering implies that the processes through which a business delivers its products or services are redesigned so that they are improved and only those parts where value is added are retained. The activity should be radical, and a clean sheet of paper approach should be adopted. Usually it involves cross-functional types of approaches; the resulting redesign often means that work flow moves onto a horizontal axis within the organization.

High Performing Teams

Companies which have undergone process re-engineering report mixed results ranging from huge success to 'disastrous' failure. Almost all have significantly reduced the number of people employed, and this has associated re-engineering with lay-offs, downsizing and redundancy.

Hammer and other champions feel that the integrity of re-engineering, and the necessity of undergoing it, remains proven by the success it has achieved when properly done. Hammer regretfully agrees that in many organizations senior management embraced re-engineering because the improvement sought was cost reduction – a means of stripping out employees. The motivation for engaging in the process should certainly be something other than cost reduction. It should seek to initiate a rethinking of the organization's processes and to redesign and regroup them in a way that serves the customer better.

Process re-engineering critics feel that the system ignores the human element and treats the people who perform the processes in a depersonalized manner. The analogy drawn is that people are handled rather as if they were machines in a production line, capable, without consequence, of being reset, reprogrammed, recalibrated to perform enlarged functions, and sometimes to be replaced entirely.

On the face of it, one would feel that teams had no part in process re-engineering. Teams after all deliver benefit from people developing synergy through their interaction with each other. Machines, even clusters of them working together, may optimize processes but they are unlikely to deliver synergy.

Reflecting a discernible defensiveness against the critical onslaught which the debate has elicited, Hammer's second book on the subject, The Reengineering Revolution Handbook (10.1), as early as its second chapter goes into the most common reasons for failure of process re-engineering initiatives, and hence the critical things to get right for it to work. He adduces the quality with which the re-engineering team does its job as the second most important success factor after leadership from the top of the organization.

The value that a cross-functional team can bring to redesigning any process is clear, and need not be rehearsed again. Hammer infers that the only way in which radical process redesign can take place successfully is as a team activity. He is also quite clear about the attributes that team must have, chief among which are those he associates with engineers in general. Engineers, he asserts, have a natural predisposition to design things, to make things and to invent. Their ability to deal with complexity and uncertainty of outcome is another benefit which he finds common in engineers and which he feels enhances the team's capability. His person specification, which he admits is simplistic, is

> 'a female engineer who has changed jobs frequently and has worked in sales'

More arresting than the claimed simplicity of the statement is the bravado of making it.

Conscious team building is also advised; Hammer gives us a neat summary of what a team should be:

- caring – of each other; respectful of different views and mutually encouraging;
- daring – innovative and adventurous;
- sharing – of objectives, of responsibility, and the roles of each other.

Much of this accords very well with our own thinking, firstly about the importance of values in teams, and secondly about the focus on process which characterizes high performing teams.

If initiating a process redesign is recommended as a team activity, it is clear from many of the applications we looked at earlier in this book that the operation of the redesigned process is also often vested in teams. Roberts Express's CATs (Customer Assistance Teams) might well be the product of a process redesign. So indeed are most of manufacturing examples, and so too are the new product development applications.

Where lies the potential difficulty which apparently besets process re-engineering and causes the heated debates and the accusations of failure? Part of the problem probably stems from the formidable complexity of redesigning all the processes within a company. Hammer also advises that the essence of success is to do it fast without encumbering the activity with huge analysis. It may be that doing fast something which is inherently so complicated may simply be too error-prone to risk.

High Performing Teams

A personal view is that process re-engineering is here to stay. It represents a valid contribution to the options available to an organization's thinking about how it should structure itself. Its potential for providing strategic advantage is far greater than simply being a way of reducing the cost base.

The contribution that teaming can make to process re-engineering is both in the initial process analysis where cross-functional applications are so materially beneficial, and in the implementation phases where high performing teams are likely to add greater value to a re-engineered process through their focus and through developing innovative rather than incremental objectives.

If the critics are right that process re-engineering fails because it is essentially a mechanistic, depersonalized process, the use of teams will redress that lacuna and, as at least some organizations have experienced, teams should help deliver the strategic benefit claimed for the process.

Building the learning organization

Why do we need learning organizations? Evidence is that organizations prosper and become mighty, get really good at what they do, and then find it very difficult to adapt to a changing environment. A survey conducted by Shell found that of the 1970 Fortune 500 companies, a third had ceased to exist by 1983.

In his important work on the phases of growth, George Ainsworth-Land (8.1) gives us a vision of a phase two company: profitable, expert, enjoying the benefit of economies of scale, and dominating its markets. The organization moves into phase three when the behaviour of its customers changes or the competitive environment in which it operates is redefined.

When this starts to happen, the silos in which organizational expertise is vested simply cannot believe that the game may have changed. Effort is spent in 'correcting' to achieve a set of conditions which formerly provided success but which may now no longer be relevant. 'Back to basics', 'stick-to-the-knitting' styles of thinking may be well advised in some circumstances, but in conditions of radical competitive redefinition they can be terminal for the organization.

Moving from a declining phase two, the pancaking S curve, to a third phase where the organization renews itself, often requires a fundamental re-evaluation of mission, purpose and potential competitive advantage. To achieve this transition we need an organization which is capable of radical re-evaluation, self-questioning, honesty and imagination. This is the learning organization. At the heart of the idea lies the thesis that organizations are parts of systems of almost unimaginable complexity.

Viewed from any specific vantage point, the visibility of the components of the system is essentially limited, and their interdependence and mutual interaction probably even more so. To manage in this unpredictable and inherently uncontrollable environment requires the organization to develop a number of areas of internal strength or capability.

Peter Senge, probably the most influential writer on learning organizations, calls these capabilities 'disciplines'. In his book The Fifth Discipline. The Art and Practice of the Learning Organization (3.6) he names them as:

- System Thinking – the ability to synthesise unrelated component parts into valid patterns which enable us to deal better with events or predict likely outcomes more accurately.
- Personal Mastery – continuously deepening, clarifying and exercising commitment around the things which are really important for the person and the organization.
- Mental Models – those things which we believe to be fundamental truths about ourselves and our organizations potentially limit our creativity and our ability to change. We need constantly to re-examine and test the veracity of these beliefs. We need to be sure that the models we are working with are appropriate but also do not exclude the possible.
- Building Shared Vision – not, as Senge says, just a 'vision statement' but a shared vision which is understood, felt, worked at and developed all the time by all the stakeholders.
- Team Learning – the ability of the team, by their consistent clarification, questioning and dialogue, to understand and grasp the significance of events faster and more accurately than could an individual.

High Performing Teams

It is absolutely plain that these disciplines can hardly be called management techniques in the same way that business process re-engineering is a technique of redesigning the flow of work through the organization. Rather, Senge's disciplines might sensibly be called components of the culture of an organization.

At the risk of drifting too far from the point, a short comment on culture is necessary; it is those beliefs that the employees have about the way in which things are done in their organization. The word 'beliefs' is key for the culture of an organization sometimes has very little to do with what the organization espouses as its values. Employees observe what is rewarded in the organization, what is punished, what is tolerated, what is ignored, and what is discussed. The way the organization acts quite clearly marks out what it considers important, and because employees are usually pretty shrewd observers, they behave in a way which supports that culture, doing the things that get rewarded and avoiding the things that get punished.

Culture emerges from an observation of the way the organization behaves; what it does, not what it says. What's more, culture is reinforced by employee behaviour, and it becomes very difficult to change because change starts only as a consequence of all employees, top to bottom, behaving differently.

Why this is all germane to the learning organization is because Senge's disciplines involve a level of culture change which organizations do not ordinarily reward, or even provide space and opportunity to embrace. In fact there hardly exists a management vocabulary to handle Senge's thinking, let alone a personal development or objective setting mechanism which can subsume it – 'I want you to improve your mental modelling by next appraisal, Fred' is unlikely to trigger purposeful behaviour change in Fred.

It is because of the lack of framework in most organizations that teaming presents a means of moving towards the learning organization. The environment of the team, especially the woo woo areas, provides an opportunity to develop some of the disciplines Senge advises. If the team is clear about the values and vision it is trying to achieve, if it does stop to evaluate how it is doing against those values, if it puts in position the feedback loops which cause it to examine how it is handling team processes – if it does these things, the team provides a forum in which the disciplines can develop.

It is simple-minded to assume that a team-type structure on its own would be sufficient to achieve a learning organization. Commitment, understanding and culture shift would have to be generated at multiple points in the organization. It might take time for people to recognize the value of what was being achieved. It would certainly be difficult to run a controlled experiment to test the concept. Teams might provide a test bed, however. Indeed I cannot see a means of developing a learning organization without structuring most of it into teams and using team development as the growth medium for learning.

Empowerment

Empowerment involves creating an environment where power, taking decisions and approving courses of action is devolved upon employees where those decisions were previously vested in managers. By providing this power to employees, and backing and supporting their resulting actions, the organization accesses different and potentially better informed sources of information which will, in turn, improve operations.

The major pay-off of empowerment, however, is that because of people's enhanced sense of value, worth or importance, the organization taps into an enhanced level of commitment from its employees. Commitment unlocks unusual effort, purposeful activity, focus on results, working both harder and smarter; it is a turbocharger of employee behaviour and it produces spectacularly improved performance. Nor is it necessary to develop an argument to defend this view. We all have personal experience of how much better we perform when we believe that there is value in what we are doing and, importantly, that the value is perceived by others and, most importantly of all, that among 'others' are our bosses.

This is what empowerment is trying to achieve. To succeed, the organization has to redistribute decision making and responsibility in ways which are not merely cosmetic but are seen by employees as genuine and of real value. Managers must behave in ways which support those people now taking the decisions, and enable their success by training, development, access and proselytizing to the rest of the organization on their behalf.

Nor is this redistribution of decision making merely delegation. Empowerment is only achieved when the organization demonstrates mutual commitment and support. This implies allowing mistakes to happen but using them to learn. It implies extending and committing to realistic time spans in which things are to happen. It implies mentoring, coaching, providing constant feedback, loose/tight involvement, keeping the predators at bay and so on. It implies creating a different organizational culture.

We have seen in some of the teaming applications that almost every time a team is set up there follows a period when it seeks to renegotiate its mandate or remit. Usually the attempt is to broaden the scope and area of responsibility. We know too that successful teams are supported by changes in the behaviour of the manager responsible for setting up the team. These activities provide the forum in which the rules and reciprocity of empowerment are established.

Most applications of empowerment utilize teams. The good reason behind this is that the support of a team 'spreads the risk' in the minds of those being empowered, to say nothing of minimizing the threat to those doing the empowering. The team environment provides an appropriate environment to debate, formulate and test drive decisions; if this is so, team decisions are likely to be better than decisions which have not been debated.

As the team's authority and accountability are progressively extended, we are in effect aiming to expand the measure of empowerment. Empowerment is not an absolute condition. We saw in the evolutionary model of self-directed teams that there can be a gradual assumption of progressive levels of responsibility as the team gains confidence and experience. What is important is that at any time there are clear agreements as to the scope of empowerment being exercised and where the limitations lie. Confusion about this can undermine the level of mutual trust which has been achieved and set back encouraging developments.

Of course empowerment is not team dependent. It is perfectly possible to empower an individual by vesting in

122

him/her enhanced levels of authority. The same mechanisms or provisos for success exist:

- clarity of purpose and agreement about scope and limitation;
- changed management behaviour to support the new locus of decision making or authority;
- training, development and enablement of the individual or team to predispose towards success.

A last observation of significance is that you will never achieve a high performing team unless it has a high degree of empowerment, authority and responsibility.

The dispersed organization

Using teams within organizations which are geographically dispersed provides special challenges. National organizations operating from multiple sites have the advantage of working in approximately the same time zones (give or take a few hours), and with employees who speak the same language and have a relatively homogeneous culture and education. International or global organizations, operating from multiple countries, possibly across 24 hours of time zones, speaking different languages and coming from a diversity of cultural bases, probably have the most challenging problem in maintaining internal communication and exchange of ideas.

Dispersed organizations need teams for the same sorts of purposes, constituted in the same way and subject to the same success factors as single site organizations. One could make a case for suggesting that dispersed organizations have a greater need of teams, and that global organizations need them even more. Singapore's input to a new product or service is as important as Chicago's.

Organizations confronting national or international project management increasingly have to draw upon teams. International customers often need levels of services which can be provided only by reciprocal international suppliers. Managing uniformity of delivery, leveraging best practice, and at the same time being sensitive to local variations usually requires an internationally constituted team to support the client relationship.

We know, however, that the synergy necessary to achieve high performance in a team is built as much from trust and mutual familiarity as it is from commonality of purpose. It usually arises from the interaction of team members getting to know one another. Technology can achieve this, but it is less effective than social interaction and it takes longer. Telephone, fax, voice mail, video-conferencing, e-mail and PC networks are all means by which the necessary interaction can be developed. Software enhancements to networks like Lotus Notes are also accelerating and improving the quality, range and depth of remote interaction by making it easier and more user-friendly, and by providing easier access to each other's work. There remains a long way to go, however, in developing software which really reflects the processes of a team at work or enables their replication in some form.

Most organizations have found that even granted a high degree of technological underpinning, high performing teams need to meet in person periodically. People communicate by a rich range of techniques, and IT can capture some of these but not all. These less frequent team meetings are often enhanced by facilitator-led development programmes, sometimes by outdoor adventure-type approaches. Structuring these meetings to gain maximum personal revelation, each of the other, pays excellent short-term dividends.

The stress here, however, is on the words 'short term'. Organizations committed to running teams which are geographically dispersed tend to find that they come together more slowly. They also seem to become high performing teams less frequently than teams in which members meet each other regularly. Sometimes dispersed teams operate well only sporadically. Sitting around a table at frequent intervals still seems to be the most effective way for a team to form and to operate.

The 'Shamrock' organization

Usually as the consequence of a strategic decision to slim down and cut costs, some organizations have reconstructed themselves, maintaining core skills and competences within. Divisions and activities which are not regarded as core, or are peripheral, though necessary, to the organization's operations, have been outsourced or subcontracted.

Teams and contemporary management trends

Sometimes they have been spun off from the original organization to become independent suppliers to their former host and other clients. This has often worked well, developing robust and efficient subcontractors usually working far more effectively than they would have if they were still part of their original establishment.

This has led to the 'shamrock' configuration, a descriptor provided for us by Charles Handy (10.2). The three leaves of the shamrock are respectively:

- the core workforce of an organization;
- the contractual fringe, those subcontractors from which the organization will purchase products and services;
- the flexible labour force – the people the host organization buys in to handle peaks of activity, overload or short-term help.

Handy estimates that one-third of Britain's workforce falls within the contractual fringe or the flexible labour force. The shamrock configuration is not then a rare phenomenon, in British organizations at least.

To operate in this environment it is necessary to form alliances, sometimes temporary, sometimes more permanent, where aggregations of organizations come together to serve a customer, each contributing component parts of a total product or service. To provide overall co-ordination and case management inevitably involves teams where members are working for different employers (some may even be employees of the client) and where the objective is the fulfilment of a contracted purchase.

It is plainly hard to develop in such a team a true commonality of purpose, even granted the best of win/win intentions. Members will have discreet organizational agendas which they may or may not be in a position to share. It is also sometimes difficult to install some of the softer-side behavioural disciplines which help build the team and accelerate it to high performance.

There is some evidence that the 'community of fate' philosophy we found at Toyota helps such teams come together. (It is just as well this is so, for it is rumoured that Toyota in Japan has some 30 000 subcontractors in its contractual fringe.) The relationship with which we are more familiar is somewhat different, however, for usually the host organization commands the strategic high ground and exercises its clout with varying degrees of benignity towards both its contractual fringe and its flexible labour force.

It is beyond doubt, however, that the future will see more and more organizations involved in different configurations of alliances with numbers of partners. Teams composed of members of different organizations will be the mechanism of project management and it will become increasingly necessary for such teams to hit high performance fast.

Performance management – MBO, Kaizen and Hoshin Kanri

Organizations survive because they identify the correct strategies and because they implement the means by which those strategies can be achieved. The sequence looks something like this:

Mission – what we do and why we do it
Vision – where we would like to be as a result of doing it
Strategy – the things we will do to get where we would like to be
Objectives – the things we need to accomplish in order to achieve the strategy
Indicators – how we will know we are getting to achieve our objectives.

This sequence matches a time scale: Mission – ongoing, Objectives – usually the annual plan, Indicators – the review periods, e.g. quarterly.

Almost all organizations plan; most extrapolate current performance to a new set of financial and fiscal objectives. They then back-fill a plan to provide the component figures. Finally they will use some sort of objective setting and appraisal system to ensure that individuals perform in accordance with the plan.

In our flatter, leaner, dispersed and process re-engineered organization, built on empowered teams, have we not done everything to assure that we spot trends early and respond with speed and imagination? Is it not reasonable to expect that our people need only be told of a new strategic direction to assure that team leaders are out of their traps like greyhounds in pursuit of the hare?

Sometimes that is OK, but most of the time it is insufficient. In general all the steps are in place; what is usually wanting is the linkage. Developing an annual plan which supports the strategic direction and is co-ordinated across the organization takes a great deal more planning work and management intervention than one would expect. We are seeing more organizations looking to balance the hands-off cultural philosophy implicit in the concept of the empowered organization with a much tighter approach to performance management. 'Performance management' here means that the implementing of the strategy is managed more tightly. The mechanism used is planning, and again the Japanese have provided a usable blueprint.

This more complex planning activity looks roughly like this:

■ First of all, abandon any idea of developing an annual plan. You are engaging in a planning exercise, the purpose of which is to achieve the vision. Trust the fact that an annual plan will emerge at the end of the process, and, incidentally, so will a substantial part of the following year's and the following . . .
■ Get really clear about the strategic intent – what are the things we will need to do to move us closer to our vision? If this sounds a bit hazy, let us not lose sight of the fact that strategic intent is pretty hard-edged. It is about what we are going to do to gain competitive advantage.
■ Determine the few, and that means few, shortfalls between where we are now and our strategic intent. Sometimes these are called the critical success factors – the gaps we must close, the things that simply must go right. Plan how we are going to do this – remember this is not 'business as usual', we are looking for breakthrough. This is the hoshin management application in Japanese.
■ Determine those parts of the operation that must simply continue to operate smoothly and drive the organization forward. These activities are the things which are probably subject to continuous incremental improvement. Many organizations subsume the planning in these areas under TQM (total quality management) activities. This is the kaizen management application.

■ Now march the plan down the organization, across it, and back up it. As it moves in each of these directions, refine and tune it. The aim is to achieve the alignment of the organization around the planning, specifically to determine:

■ What parts of the breakthrough can we achieve and by when – how will we measure it? What we will have to do to achieve it.

■ What will constitute incremental improvement – how will we measure it? What we will have to do to achieve it.

■ Last, institute the review and audit procedure – many organizations use Deming's PDCA (Plan, Do, Check, Act) cycle. The Plan and Do parts of the process are the review activity. The Check and Act parts of it are the audit process – did it work? has the target moved?

This sort of planning has become known by the general name of Hoshin Kanri and the analogies offered for it are implicit in the meaning of the words. Hoshin loosely translated means a compass, kanri means planning. In other words the process provides a navigational system for the organization.

A number of important organizations are claimed to be using Hoshin Kanri: Hewlett-Packard, Intel, Texas Instruments, to name a few. Extravagant claims are made for its success.

Among the preconditions for high performing teams, as we have seen, is absolute clarity about objectives. This kind of planning and high performance team development show a wonderfully compatible relationship. Couple the benefits of high performing teams to an organizational planning process designed to gain alignment, and you have the potential for a highly effective management system.

Teams and competence

In the UK and the USA 'competence' means subtly different things. The UK has chosen to apply the concept to the whole process of vocational training, education and development. The National Council for Vocational Qualifications has commissioned and approved a large number of occupational areas to develop generic competencies related to various levels of expertise. It has linked evidence of competence to qualification and extended this to certification. Thus a person capable of providing evidence of competence against one of these independently developed sets of generic standards may gain a transferable qualification from an independent awarding body. Many millions have been spent on this enterprise and vocational qualifications have become a cornerstone of government education and training policy.

In the USA competence has flowed more out of the assessment centre movement. Again, definitions of generic and specific competences are established in relation to certain job roles. The definitions tend to be couched in behavioural terms and individuals are assessed by demonstrating their ability to satisfy these definitions. Much of the assessment is based on simulation.

The rest of the world lines up with either the UK or the US schools of thought. No universally agreed sets of competency exist, and even those countries which tend more towards the highly definitive UK practice do not necessarily rely on the UK competence definitions but have sometimes developed their own.

In all applications, however, it is the competence of the individual which is being assessed. By and large, no generally agreed set of competences has been developed or universally accepted for the team. The implicit assumption is that the competence of the team leader, coupled with the collective competences of individual members of the team, will determine the team's performance.

More recently, excellent work has been done by a number of consultants who have developed competence definitions for differing kinds of teams in specific organizational environments. Some of this appears to have flowed out of training needs analyses. In other words, in order to determine how we will train the team to achieve high performance, we need first to determine what constitutes high performance in the specific organizational environment in which this team operates.

Interesting reports are starting to emerge which appear to have moved on somewhat from the traditional Belbin (and others) models of team roles. The best of this work defines competence and then expands the definition by rendering it into specific behavioural descriptors. This can be further assisted by outlining both the positive behaviours, those that contribute towards the competence, and negative behaviours, those that inhibit. Since, as we know, much of which makes a team effective and incipiently high performing is the nature and quality of the interaction between its members, rendering competence into recognizable behaviour seems particularly helpful to team members and seems to accelerate team development.

On the face of it, if we are able to identify those things that produce high performance in a specific organizational environment and then render these into competence and behavioural definitions, we should have unlocked access to a powerful set of tools. Those who advocate the superiority of this approach over the use of generic competence definitions adduce the following advantages.

- We can define competences to address the specific culture of the organization in which the team is working.
- We can define competences in terms which relate directly to the organization's strategic intent.
- We can define competences in terms of the specific systems that the organization employs.

All this is true; there is no question that if members of a team are supported by access to competences which have achieved high performance in their organization in the past, then their development can be a great deal more targeted and directed.

The argument seems to turn on the degree to which behavioural definitions are used to amplify the competences. The need to be specific about positive or negative behaviour is probably a function of the sophistication of the members of the team and the degree of information to which they have access. Put rather crassly, if team members are capable of predicating the marketing strategy of the organization, they probably are bright enough to be able to define and produce behaviour that supports it and avoid behaviour that does not.

In summary, competence systems are tools or techniques by which high performance can be accelerated. To the best of my knowledge no specific team-based generic competences exist though they feature as subsets of many of the UK's occupationally defined generic systems. Consultants are quite good at developing them for specific organizational environments and this seems to benefit team development.

Teams and Leadership

Thinking, research and practice in the subject of leadership probably accounts for a substantial chunk of the enormous management literature that cascades annually from the book and periodical publishers. Most of this work seeks to determine what sort of things a leader/manager should do to help his/her organization to survive in turbulent and unpredictable times. Increasingly too, the focus is on developing a leadership model which helps to sustain and optimize teams and team-based organizational structures.

We have already seen in Chapter 8 on setting up teams that there is no clear specification for successful leadership within a team. It is probably also true to say that the nature of the leadership qualities needed to achieve high performance in the team are probably not the same as those needed to sustain it.

We have also seen in Chapter 6 that managers who are responsible for the team's interactions within the rest of the organization must sustain radical changes in their accustomed or usual behaviour and activities. The task is optimizing the team's operating environment rather than the traditional decision and control based management activities.

Because I have worked a lot with it, I personally favour the model developed by Wilson Learning in its Leader-Manager training programmes. Its strength lies in that it:

- focuses strongly on the individual employee's agenda and priorities and helps reconcile these with organizational imperatives;
- creates a strong and supportive environment for devolved decision taking, empowerment and hence team building;
- does not abdicate the managerial responsibility for results.

Perhaps this model is best encapsulated in Wilson's Leader-Manager Balance (10.3).

High Performing Teams

The Leader-Manager Balance

Leadership	Management
Addresses 'why'	Addresses 'how'
Inspiration	Clarification
Service Focus	Profit Focus
Strategy	Operations
Innovation	Improvement
Fulfilment	Performance
Versatility	Consistency
Alignment	Accountability

It is the role of the manager to strike the most appropriate balance between these two visions. 'Most appropriate' is affected by the organization and its culture, the employees and their competencies, the responsibilities of the manager, and, last but by no means least, the competitive environment in which the organization operates.

It hardly needs saying, however, that if empowered, high performing teams are the aim, management practice will tend more to the left-hand column than to the right.

Executive summary

Management trend	What it means	How teams relate to trend
Business process re-engineering	• Redesigning the processes through which the business delivers its products and services • Work flows horizontally through organization • Usually 'right- or downsizing'	• Redesign is a team activity • The better the team, the better the re-engineering • Cross-functional teams usually operate redesigned process

Building the learning organization	• Creating a culture in which the organization learns from its mistakes and does so faster
	• Employs Senge's five disciplines:
	  System Thinking
	  Personal Mastery
	  Mental Models
	  Shared Vision
	  Team Learning
		• Teams become the units of learning in the organization
		• Team processes (especially woo woo) favour the development of the five disciplines

Empowerment	• Devolves power (decisions and approvals) from managers to others • Enables better informed decisions and better buy-in	• Team often (usually) the unit in which power is vested • Teams debate, formulate and 'test drive' decisions
Dispersed organizations	• Multi-site – multinational • Problems in team development because of difficulty of 'getting round the table'	• For multinationals – teams facilitate global input • Teams needed to assure uniformity of customer experience and best practice etc.
Shamrock organizations	• Organization is small cluster of skills – non-core activities outsourced • Cuts operating costs and allows access to broader expertise	• Teams control and project manage disparate suppliers • Client can/should be part of the team • New win/win solutions may be needed
Performance management – MBO, Kaizen and Hoshin Kanri	• Institutes different planning procedures • Permits organization to navigate to achieve strategic intent • Produces both continuous improvement and organizational breakthrough • Creates strategically relevant objectives	• Teams become the implementation nodes for each critical success factor • Teams determine own objectives in light of critical success factors and hence strategy • Quality circle and task force type team activity

High Performing Teams

Management trend	What it means	How teams relate to trend
Competence	• Tries to define activities and behaviours which achieve success • Uses as basis for training and development	• No agreed generic competences for team success • Recent consultancy has defined specific team in specific organization competencies • Behavioural interpretation helps team development
Leadership	• Attempts to define what makes good leaders when . . . . . . environment is turbulent and unpredictable . . . structures are 'non traditional'	• Teams are increasingly the unit of organizational structure • Leader role increasingly to provide appropriate organizational environment in which team can operate • Balance of leader/manager behaviour required

11 Teams and the future

This chapter looks at five factors which will dominate the organizational environment of the future. It describes why each factor is important, how it might affect the organization and how it will relate to teams.

The modern organization

We have spent a lot of time in this book talking of the changed competitive climate in which organizations operate. The contemporary manager/practitioner deals on a daily basis with concerns about change, competitiveness, discontinuity and unpredictability. Many managers, if not most, have presided over organizational initiatives to shed cost, create flatter and more responsive organizations, and to get closer to the customer.

As a result, the structure of the modern organization is more likely to have a strong reliance on team-based operating units. It is likely to be more people-focused than it was a decade ago and it will be looking to its staff to behave in a participative and contributory manner. In return it will be extending developmental opportunities to its employees both by way of formal learning and by the increasing scope of responsibility and empowerment.

The organization will be a lot more productive than it was a decade ago and many of its previous functions may now be outsourced. It will probably be clustering its activities around a group of what it sees as its core skills; usually those things wherein, it believes, lie its competitive advantages.

If that is where we are now, what are the things that are most likely to change the face of work in the future?

High Performing Teams

Futurology is notoriously prone to error, and only a few sages like Drucker and the Tofflers have proven the viability of visions which, when they were first predicated, might have seemed at best alarmist and at worst bizarre. There are a few trends which will have a transforming effect, and it might be helpful to look at their impact on the organization and the team of the future.

Here are those things which I think will affect us most:

Information technology
Hypercompetition
Organizational responsiveness
Post-modern values
Learning

Teams and information technology

As the man said: 'You ain't seen nothing yet.' Much as IT has changed the face of modern organizations, it is reasonable to expect that its impact will be more universally and more fundamentally felt in the future. Newer technologies like artificial intelligence, neurocomputing, nanotechnology, plus enhancements in telecommunications, coupled with improving user friendliness and falling prices, will generate rafts of applications which most of us have yet to dream of. This issue is less about easier access to information or even about having more information. What will change is the way IT helps us solve the problem of the excess of information: The way data is organized, the way it enables patterns to be recognized, the way complexity can be simplified and systems of useful synthesis imposed on mere data.

Developments in IT will affect the way work is done, where it is done, who does it, and what that work is. It will also generate entirely new industries and it will transform the Fortune 500 even more radically than it has been transformed over the past twenty years.

What bearing will this have on teams and teaming? A few ideas . . .

Increasingly information will not only inform, but will actually be the major differentiator between organizations. The evolution and deployment of the strategies to achieve this is going to be the work of teams because hierarchies are simply too ponderous and unresponsive to be effective.

The ability of high performing teams to process and assess more information reliably and with greater effectiveness will make them more necessary to interpret the huge amount of disparate data to which the organization will have access. The multiple perspectives of cross-functionality will be increasingly important in decision making.

It is to be hoped that really excellent software, shareware or teamware will be developed (see 'The Dispersed Organizations' in Chapter 10). This software will enable people in locations remote from each other and in different time zones to replicate the processes of a team meeting. The software will enable Senge-type discourse, it will convey nuance and tone, it will stimulate creativity, it will enable scenarios to be modelled quickly and simulated effectively, and it will facilitate the reaching of consensus.

If the past provides any reliable basis for extrapolation into the future, IT may be the source of additional complexity, or it may contribute to the resolution of it. The human filter will remain the ultimate bridge between information and action. It is my view that the filter is likely to a collective one, a team.

Teams and hypercompetition – achieving strategic versatility

Strategy is about winning wars, not about winning battles. What a company seeks in pursuit of its strategy is to create sustainable competitive advantage. The tablets of stone in which thinking about strategy is codified come from Harvard and are brought to us by Michael Porter in his important and influential 1980 book Competitive Strategy (11.1). Porter suggests that there are three generic strategies that a company can pursue:

- cost leadership – being a low-cost producer and hence having greater flexibility to price one's product or service;
- differentiation – providing a wide (the widest) range of products and services;

- focus – dominating a sector of the market with one of the above and innovating to maintain the domination of that sector.

Importantly Porter warned that to pursue more than one of the options above might lead a company to be immobilized by the conflicting organizational and marketing requirements each strategy required to sustain it.

Few management theories, even those of the intellectual excellence of Porter's, survive a decade; there is now some evidence to suggest that some companies have actually managed to pursue both cost leadership and differentiation strategies simultaneously. Also emerging is a view that competitive advantage derives equally from a set of unique core capabilities that an organization must develop.

From Richard D'Aveni (11.2) comes not only the word hypercompetition (which I find useful since it changes the way we think about the contemporary competitive environment) but also a view that strategic advantage cannot be maintained. Instead it must be gained and regained as an organization successively achieves it, loses it to a competitor, and then wins it back. D'Aveni warns that the pursuit of traditional strategies 'can be a deadly distraction'. Among his suggestions is that the only viable strategy to pursue is one of constant disruption of the markets so that competitors are constantly caught on the back foot and forced into catch-up mode.

Whatever one's views in the above debate, there is evidence to suggest that organizations will have to be able to pursue multiple strategies simultaneously. Furthermore, because the durability of any single strategy is likely to be limited, the organization must continuously re-invent its strategic advantages in an environment where the competition is just as active and potentially engaged in the same activity.

One thing is certain: the lack of strategic direction within a company has been terminal in the past and it is likely that it will continue to be so in the future. Even a mistaken strategy is less damaging than none at all since you usually have the ability to correct mistakes provided you spot them early enough.

Given that high performing teams aggregate around clear sets of objectives, it is potentially possible for an organization to run simultaneous strategies side by side, vesting responsibility for the different sets of results implicit in each strategy within different sets of teams. Plainly this might require duplication of infrastructure and resources, but at least teams provide a viable means of playing on two or more fronts simultaneously and hence addressing Porter's warning of the dangers of pursuing mixed strategies. This ability to play on more than one front simultaneously is what I call strategic versatility.

We see some of this in companies that place the management of given brands in the hands of different teams. Sometimes the range of brands that the organization is handling may in part be competitive. In the past this has proved a dubiously successful business, but given the unpredictability of competitors and the rapid changes possible in consumer behaviour, it is a conceivable strategy, if not a necessary one, that the company of the future will try to cover a number of bases simultaneously.

Since it is arguably the most important function of any organization, strategy formulation can no longer be relegated (and now rarely is) to the responsibility of a separate department of the company. It has become the business of the whole company as represented by teams capable of delivering accurate and relevant input, taking informed, cross-functional decisions, and generating the conviction and the buy-in which are the necessary pre-cursors for implementation.

Organizational responsiveness – creating the athletic organization

That implementation too depends on a management system which cascades strategy and the objectives associated with it down the organization and, as importantly, across it too. Increasingly, cross-functional and overlapping teams are the structural components through which strategy implementation drives the resulting organizational change. Each team becomes a node aligning and developing its own strategy with the bigger company picture, and then defining its objectives from that strategic base. (See the Hoshin Kanri explanation in the previous chapter.)

High Performing Teams

Henry Mintzberg, the sage of how organizations structure themselves, has given us, in the 1970s and 1980s, six patterns of organizational structure. Each of these models is suited particularly to a given type of business and a given type of environment in which that business operates. Furthermore, each structure has, at its heart, a co-ordinating principle which makes it operate properly. While not wanting to recapitulate Mintzberg's work here, a couple of examples might help.

At one end of the scale we have the 'machine' organizational structure, which operates well for a business engaged in mass production in a relatively stable environment. The use of the word 'machine' implies the pattern of the organization's structure: a series of interlocking components each with a specific function. The co-ordinating principle is the standardization of work processes.

At the other end of the scale is the so-called 'adhocracy', suited to the provision of complex products and services in an environment that changes rapidly. Its co-ordinating principle is face-to-face meetings between groups of people. Again the word 'adhocracy' describes the underlying organizational principle: high flexibility and versatility of the operating components.

Perhaps the most memorable business aspects of the 1980s and 1990s is the degree to which organizations have shed labour. White- and blue-collar workforces have both been affected, and the move has been worldwide. It is unlikely that organizations will ever re-inflate to vitiate the productivity per capita improvements they have so painfully achieved. If organizations ever conformed to Mintzberg's principles, that conformity has been radically affected by the depredations of 'rightsizing', de-layering, business process re-engineering, resource-based theory and so on. The practice of shedding people and cost has not come to an end; nor will it ever.

What is emerging, and likely to become the standard rather than the exception, is mixed structures which relate more to the underlying strategy and objectives. Thus we might have a classic Mintzberg machine-based structure operating services while a Mintzberg adhocracy dealt with clients.

Whether called by that name or not, most organizations have critical success factors – those things that absolutely have to go right if corporate objectives are to be achieved. Businesses tend increasingly to organize their activities around component parts which are capable of delivering those critical success factors. Cross-functional teams are the usual means of achieving this.

As we saw in the description of Hoshin Kanri and its interaction with Kaizen, balancing breakthrough with continuous improvement means that a team-based structure is more likely to provide the speed of organizational response which will increasingly be at a premium.

A high degree of co-ordination is, of course, a prerequisite of the system, but it is also easy to see how an organizational structure of overlapping teams would be in a position to respond relatively fast to major changes of direction or minor changes of tactics. This starts to convey a picture of how organizational athleticism might be achieved: robust operating units capable of quick response and providing rapid changes of direction.

Teaming will also play an increasingly important part in the new organization where previously integral services have been spun off or contracted out. For these shamrock organizations to operate they must be supported by clusters of subcontractors and sometimes part-time workers. Here, as we have seen, the behavioural mechanisms which characterize high performing teams are a useful model by which disparate entities can come together to focus on a project. Part-timers, subcontractors and full-time company employees can more rapidly 'hit stride' if participants are familiar with, and open to, team-based operating principles.

The need to change organizations fast, to stop them in mid-stride and turn them without missing a beat seems to me an essential attribute of the future organization. To achieve this organizational anatomy, structure, and organizational physiology (how it operates), must change. Concerns about how to put together the component parts and then to enliven them with an effective management system will dominate the future. Teams are likely to provide part of the answer to both halves of the problem.

Post-modern values

When J. Edwards Deming was asked what he had learned about his extensive international experience, particularly that which he had gained in Japan, he is reputed to have made the laconic reply, 'people are important'. People too are changing. We look to a future where the employee or worker is different from the traditional blue- or white-collar model which has dominated most of the twentieth century.

First of all, the use of the word 'worker' rather than employee is significant, for in many cases, as we have seen, the service may be provided by somebody outside or only temporarily inside the organization. Charles Handy's shamrock organization, the clover leaf structure, envisages a core of employees dealing with a far larger constituency of providers from whom services are bought. So the philosophy of the organization buying a person's labour is replaced by a new relationship in which the organization makes a limited (the outside supplier) or continuous (the employee) purchase of service. One should add that even the word 'continuous' probably requires the qualificatory prefix of 'relatively'.

The worker too is, and will increasingly be, better educated and trained, more aware of the need to continue to learn and develop in order to maintain or enhance his/her market value. Security of relationship is more likely to be achieved by high performance than by any organizational paternalism which may have protected employees in the past. Where employers are offering a degree of security, it will be offered more in the context of the 'community of fate' concept we encountered in the Toyota case.

What organizations will not be able to afford is to treat individuals as component parts of a machine in the best Theory X management traditions. To attract the shifting population of good minds and experience for which they will be competing, organizations will have to place their people in environments of high reward. This obviously has to do with money, but it has also to do with the ability to gain experience, to train, to contribute and to exercise responsibility. These environments are going to look more like teams than hierarchies.

It is fair to say that the effect of post-modern values on the organization will be more far-reaching than merely in its relationships with its employees. The Royal Society of Arts inquiry Tomorrow's Company (2.3) speaks of the 'death of deference' (to the company) so that it is now challenged not only by its competitors and its marketplace, the needs of its customers, its employees and its investors, but also by an increasing constituency of stakeholders who collectively endorse what the study calls a company's 'licence to operate'. This licence is earned by the company's ability to satisfy public opinion and to create confidence both in the company and in the industry in which it operates. It must deal with the power of the media and the political establishment. It needs to satisfy the agendas of a range of pressure groups and lobbies which can often mobilize to frustrate corporate intention at extremely short notice and to increasing effect. Finally it must satisfy the law, regulatory mechanisms and industry and market standards.

The philosophy of the 'licence to operate' seems to me to imply a compounding of the complexity of the organizational environment. People, and more effectively, people in teams, are going to be the means of unravelling that complexity and the means by which the resulting organizational changes will be most swiftly enacted.

Teams and learning – providing the organization with intellectual humility

It is virtually impossible to write about organizational or individual learning without sounding pious and trite about the need for life-long learning, continuous professional development etc. We all know that the shelf life of our formal professional education is pretty short; we all know we live in the information age, and an increasing number of us work in fast-paced knowledge industries. The case for individuals to take responsibility for their learning and development hardly needs to be made.

Providing access to continuous learning means that the way in which it is delivered and the agents who deliver it are likely to change even more quickly than they have in the past. The divide between the formal education establishment (universities, polytechnics, colleges, business schools), the professional bodies, and finally the corporate entities is likely to become less clear as each has to operate in the service of the other.

The process of resolving the sometimes differing agendas of academic standards, professional standards, and the competences that the organization deems appropriate to its strategic intention is not necessarily easy. Agreeing the learner developmental activities and assessment systems which will satisfy all three sets of stakeholders, and finally delivering these programmes, provides a further level of complexity and cost which can frustrate the corporate paymaster. Nonetheless this fusion of academic, professional and organizational agendas is increasingly being achieved with success.

Researchers in the business schools are producing a lot of helpful work determining the conditions in which all members of the organization are enabled to learn. Foremost among these is Peter Senge with his Fifth Discipline (3.6) – a must for any manager really taking his/her job seriously. Pedlar, Burgoyne and Boydell's more recent collection Towards the Learning Company: Concepts and Practices (11.3) is an engaging and useful contribution to the manager seeking to provide the climate and systems which assist employees to learn.

In the section 'Building the Learning Organization' (Chapter 10), we looked at Senge's five disciplines and some of the culture changes that would be necessary to install them in an organization. In addition, the organization will increasingly have to provide both the formal education and training mentioned above and the opportunity for informal learning gained in observing, measuring, experimenting and concluding, from the actual daily practice of the company in operation. The company is a dynamic system, and even a small organization is hugely complex, affected by thousands of variables only some of which are in the control of those who operate it. Learning to understand and manipulate the levers that will affect company performance is plainly a vital form of learning, and, as we saw in the 'Building the Learning Organization' section, frequently a critical component of strategic renewal.

This kind of organizational wisdom has historically been invested in experience. Older employees, senior managers and experienced operatives have successfully steered the organization in times which were relatively more predictable, or at least changing less swiftly. The new environment outlined at the start of this chapter, an environment of discontinuous and unpredictable change, has meant that new forms of learning must now steer the company through the turbulent contemporary currents of competition.

Teams and the future

Knowledge and understanding obviously still reside in the heads of the company's employees and not in some suprahuman collective entity – least of all the IT system. Senge sheds great insight into the singular contribution of team learning when he uses Heisenberg's description of the power of conversation to formulate, clarify, and contribute towards the thinking of others. What a team does in open exchange and discussion is to create a process for the accelerated interpretation and understanding of events. The effect is to:

> 'illustrate the staggering potential of collaborative learning – that collectively, we can be more insightful, more intelligent than we can possibly be individually. The IQ of the team can, potentially, be much greater than the IQ of the individuals.'

To achieve the kind of team learning being described here, and for the company to be able to avail itself of the benefit it can contribute, conscious provision needs to be made to develop and reward team learning. Space must be provided for the team to reflect on what it has learned. The internal dynamics of the team's functions must allow for open discussion, and an environment must be provided in which unorthodox opinion or uncomfortable revelations are not derided and excluded but seriously entertained for their contribution to collective enlightenment.

If the unit of company learning and company wisdom is increasingly the team, the fuel of team learning is a high octane blend of trust, mutual respect of members, and permission for the individual to go out on a limb without threat.

Hickman and Silva in their 1987 book entitled The Future 500 (11.4) provide an interesting construct of the future management scenario. They call it complexity management and it requires:

■ gaining perspective through identifying the unifying principles behind the inherently complex environment in which organizations operate (Senge calls this System Thinking);
■ providing freedom to act – essentially this is the empowerment philosophy;
■ providing individual fulfilment – this really addresses the post-modern needs of the employee and, probably through the ethical conformity of the organization, the investor as well.

High Performing Teams

This book tries (rather too) hard to pack a lot of disparate material into the confined scope of complexity management; it does however endorse a future view of people-led rather than system-led organizations. I remain convinced that the unit of leadership is far more likely to be teams of people.

Executive summary

The High Performing Team	
. . . What it does/will do	**. . . Organizational benefit it provides**

	. . . What it does/will do	. . . Organizational benefit it provides

Effect of burgeoning IT applications:
  – what work is done
  – the way it is done
  – where it is done
	• Is able to process large amounts of data
	• Cross-functionality provides multiple perspective and reliable interpretation
		• Better informed decisions
		• Faster decisions
		• Hence faster response

Effects of hypercompetition	• Helping determine strategy provides buy-in • Teams manage individual 'brand' • Multiple teams manage multiple, part-competing brands	• Allows more than one strategy to be pursued • Does not beggar one strategy in favour of another • Accelerates implementation of strategic change
Need for organizational responsiveness . . . creating the athletic organization	• Organizes activities to achieve critical success factors (CSFs) • Allocates CSFs across the organization • Accommodates Hoshin and Kaizen implementation • Deals with subcontractors and part-timers	• Provides a management system for implementation of change • Accelerates speed with which the company can change • Improves company flexibility
Effect of post-modern values	• Provides appropriate environment for the new worker • Allows personal development	• Gains access to best brains • Maintains small core of high value employees
Teams and learning – intellectual humility	• By 'discourse', accelerates understanding and interpretation of events • Becomes the unit of company learning	• More rapid response • Unlocks more imagination and ingenuity • Broadens the 'wisdom base' of the company

Semi-SWOT analysis

This chapter takes team applications that we have looked at and provides a quick evaluation of each – strengths, weaknesses and risks.

We have explored a number of facets of the team debate looking at types of teams, applications, developing and sustaining teams, how they fit with contemporary management thinking, and where they are likely to go in the future.

What the following shorthand tables try to do is not a SWOT analysis in the true sense of using that valuable tool, but rather to provide a shorthand set of reference statements which will trigger thoughts in the mind of the manager considering the upsides and downsides of introducing or expanding the use of teaming in an organization. Hopefully the thinking these tables generate will enable the manager to compile his/her own SWOT analysis and, perhaps even more germane, a realistic risk analysis.

Remember:

- Building a high performing team will always take more time than you imagine. That means elapsed time from set-up to high performance but also management's time and energy.
- Starting the process and failing is about the worst scenario. You can pilot teaming but you cannot fail at it. If you are going to do it you must succeed. Be prepared to mobilize adamantine resolve, to sustain bitter attacks (see 'Storming . . .', Chapter 9), to bind wounds and to break heads to achieve high performance. You had better believe that it is worth it . . .!

High Performing Teams

Type of team/ application	Strengths	Weaknesses	Risks if mismanaged
Task force (most widely used form)	• Limited focus provides for better solutions • Cross-functionality gets better solutions • Members' development	• Slow start-up (four stages of development)	• Can go on for ever if not pressed to conclude

Quality circle type team – continuous improvement of processes, systems and products	• Practical solutions because members come from the coalface
	• Easier implementation of change because of buy-in of members
	• Develops customer focus (internal and external)
		• Management time needed – cross-selling in the organization
		• Managers need to change style
		  – 'on the outside looking in'
		  – 'manager as gopher'
			• Team can:
			  – over-engineer process improvement
			  – 'over-satisfy' the customer

Project teams – develop new products, services, or sometimes strategies	• Organization draws on a broader base of expertise • Creativity (if asked for) can be unlocked • Buy-in because it is invented here	• Time taken for team to hit stride • Membership; needs to balance eligibility and suitability (see step 5)	• 'The lunatics take over the asylum'

Teams used as the building blocks of the organization – e.g.
– converting existing departmental structural units into teams, or
– restructuring, e.g. after process re-engineering
	• New impetus – new kick-start imparted
	• Opportunity to redefine objectives on more appropriate basis
	• Effect of empowerment is usually positive:
	  – unleashes energy
	  – stimulates creativity
	• Ultimately provides a more responsive organization
	• Enhances planning effectiveness (Kaizen/Hoshin)
		• Disorientation of staff
		• Refusal to be empowered – see Royal Mail
		• If (as it usually is) associated with downsizing, survivors feel guilty
			• Flops because seen as flavour of the day
			• Culture change, needed everywhere in the organization to sustain it, cannot be delivered

Product/Service design and development teams Cross-functional teams design new products and services	• Broad base of input means fewer launch glitches
	• Creativity (if asked for) can be unlocked
	• Enthusiasm generated around product/service design
		• Start-up time needed – 4 stages
		• Need to change membership to reflect:
		  – stage of design
		  – scope of design: extension or enhancement
			• Can step outside company strategy constraints
			• Camels – horses designed by committees

chapter 12

Semi-SWOT analysis

Type of team/ application	Strengths	Weaknesses	Risks if mismanaged
Manufacturing teams Use of cell technology - team has complete responsibility – quality and workflow – for making a component	• Cost savings/Product-ivity enhancement • Multi-skilling • Accountability – Community of fate (see Toyota)	• Re-tooling and plant layout costs • Maintaining vertical career progression • May have to provide employment guarantees	• Beware labour unions
Customer service teams Re-engineering so that all elements of customer contact and support are handled by one group Case management teams	• Improves customer focus and customer satisfaction • Often produces process/service/product improvement • Enhances organizational awareness of customer and competitor shifts	• Potential loss of some functional control • Sometimes an attendant re-organization cost – IT or facilities • Disorientation of staff because of reorganization	• Customer can get disorientated • Team can 'give the shop away'
Specialist teams – numerous applications where specialized functional or support services are developed and provided to the organization at large	• Since the focus/objectives are usually unique, team generates high interest and energy • Enables organization to create specialist cells valuable for staff development, R&D and special projects	• Perceptions of elitism and special privilege • Employees resent using internal specialists	• Organization becomes smug, too inward looking • Drift into inappropriate areas of activity or levels of abstraction – silos

Other important things to think about

This chapter suggests the things to consider (in addition to the ten steps) in setting up teams. It asks whether teaming will fit the organization, gives advice on timing, how to sell the idea internally and how to use external help. Provides a questionnaire to help thinking about and planning a move to teaming.

Other factors to consider

Earlier we dealt with the steps needed to set up a high performing team and we outlined what needs to be done to develop and sustain its performance. What this chapter will look at is some other factors a manager will need to consider when embarking on a commitment to introduce or expand teaming in the organization.

Much of the following advice comes from those who have been involved in implementation either as line managers or as consultants and trainers who have worked on team implementation processes.

It must also be said that this chapter is useful only for those managers who are attempting to build high performing teams. This implies that the intention behind moving to teaming is to tap levels of performance, flexibility, creativity and speed of response which have not been accessed before. It also means that the manager has decided to create empowered or self-directed teams because it is only by building towards increasing levels of empowerment (see chart on page 43) that the synergy characteristic of high performing teams will be unlocked.

In our Ten Steps process we advise getting clear about the problem(s) in need of solution. We also suggest that we satisfy ourselves that teaming is the best or only solution. Perhaps some of the bulleted statements in the Semi-SWOT will help reach the decision. Some more considerations are discussed below and a questionnaire follows which should enable you to do a frank and informative assessment.

Is teaming going to fit into this organization?

In implementing teaming, or in using the concepts behind it as a managerial tool, a new strain is being introduced into the organizational culture. Potentially what might happen is:

- The organization, ever resistant to disequilibrium, will attack and kill off the new strain. It must be said that this scenario is pretty common. Its manifestation is that the team or teams become grounded at levels well below high performance. They may continue to operate, but they will be delivering little that could not have been achieved simply by scheduling regular meetings.
- The new strain may be so successful that it will take over at consequent cost to the existing culture. This scenario is far less common although it does happen. The dismantling of the old culture can be expensive in people and money, and if it is not well managed, the organization can falter while it gets itself sorted out.
- The new strain will be subsumed into the existing culture and the two will live side by side. In my experience this is usually the way in which the first scenario above is represented to the world and it is often a spurious disguise cloaking a failed intent.

Most organizations are actually looking to achieve the second scenario. Not only is that the objective, but it is usually the strategic intent, a longer-term need which the organization wants to meet. If it is not, then serious consideration should be given to the idea that it should be because, as we have seen, achieving high performance is costly, time consuming and disruptive. It is hardly worth doing unless the pay-off is considerable.

It is important to realize that if the organization has developed teaming and is reaping the benefits of high performance, it is culturally very different from a successful hierarchically structured organization. The question then arises as to whether it can continue to use them properly. The advice is that in assessing the potential fit of teaming with the organization, use a long time frame.

Timing

There is evidence that the turbulence and unpredictability of the 1990s, a world recession and a slow climb back, has left many organizations pretty stressed. Where this evidence is reported, two major factors appear to emerge:

- Employees, having witnessed the 'rightsizing' activities of their own and other organizations over the recent past, no longer feel any sense of job security. Nor has the 'community of fate' philosophy we encountered at Toyota provided an alternative sense of permanence or security.
- In many organizations employees also feel exhausted or battered by constantly having to undergo changes in the way things are done, in the way the organization is structured, and in their shifting objectives. They see themselves as working harder, and forseeably having to work harder still. The new paradigm of change being the only constant has not provided a credible principle on which to build careers or sometimes even to sustain day-to-day operations.

In these conditions, enacting change becomes more difficult because the energy of the organization is depleted and its levels of cynicism are raised, producing in the staff a sort of weary compliance rather than enthusiastic commitment. You can start off on the former, but to succeed you will need to go to the afterburner power provided by the latter.

The good news is that teaming helps to address the sort of alienation described above because of the sense of belonging and participation it develops among individuals. The bad news is that the stages of developing high performing teams, particularly the storming stage, can be pretty gruelling because of the high potential for interpersonal conflict. You need a robust group to sustain this sort of stress.

Perhaps of equal importance is the question whether the manager(s) developing the team(s) have the reserves of energy, the patience and the commitment to help their teams through the stressful conditions they will encounter.

It is hard to identify a right time to enact the sweeping changes that the widespread introduction of teaming in an organization will cause. The converse is easier, however; it is relatively simple to identify the wrong time. That time is when the organization is exhausted, depleted, licking its wounds, angry and mistrustful. Teaming may not turn the tide, although of all major organizational change initiatives, it is the one most likely to start to knit the organization together again.

Selling teaming upwards in the organization

Most teaming initiatives arise from upper management, though usually not from top management. It makes sense to develop a strategy to gain the support of top management.

On the face of it this is a tough sale to make:

- It is going to take time, 12–24 months to reach high performance.
- It might not work; the teams may never become high performing.
- It could be expensive; sometimes an IT cost, facilities, training, meeting costs etc.
- There is an opportunity cost, e.g. managers' time; it is possible the organization might lose momentum before positive effects kick in.
- There could be blood on the walls as we go through the storming stages.

High Performing Teams

■ There are potentially disquieting issues surrounding control; empowered teams are only empowered by the devolution of responsibility to them. Those who are devolving responsibility onto a team probably need to be supported in their decision to do so.

The pay-offs on the other hand are delayed, speculative, and often woolly: flexibility, creativity, improved problem solving, speed of response, committed and happier employees. This is an easily dismissable bill of goods, especially when they cannot be guaranteed.

Given this apparent imbalance of risk and result, it is surprising that the upward sale is ever made. The fact that so many organizations are moving towards teaming, that so much is published and reported about it, and finally that so much is claimed for it, actually makes this sale easier. A picture of an intriguingly different environment can be painted, a robust and empowered culture can be described. Often these factors weigh more than a highly quantified business case.

However the sale is made, perhaps the most important condition to negotiate is the time span to achievement. Many, many teaming initiatives have failed because the organization simply could not hang in there long enough. Few fail if the management, top and senior, can mobilize the resources and, above all, the resolve to succeed.

Readiness to accept help

We already know that organizations implementing major teaming initiatives rely heavily upon outside help, consultants, trainers, the great outdoors etc. We also know that two types of training are necessary for the team: functional training to teach members the business skills being asked of them and team development skills to help develop the team more quickly.

The functional training required is probably specific to individuals; members will come to the team with varied levels of expertise and skills. The intention is really to provide the solid business skills necessary for them to operate effectively. Areas like problem solving, risk analysis, project management, budgeting etc. should be considered in the light of their appropriateness to the team's functions and the needs and experience of the individual members. If the opportunity arises for the team to receive joint training in any functional disciplines, so much the better; it is not usually a precondition of high performance though.

In the area of team development, however, the team must undergo development activities collectively and as an intact team. Passing the team development role backwards and forwards between the organization, say the manager responsible, and outside trainers seems to work well.

This kind of parallel track might, for example, look like this:

Manager activity (sometimes the team leader)	*Outside trainer role*
• Commission team and agree operating remit: – Mission/vision/values	• Training in team roles and how teams work: – How mission /vision/values work
• Start to develop: – Team objectives – Criteria for measuring achievement – Critical success factors – Feedback loops	• Process/technique-based sessions aimed at: – Achieving agreement/alignment – Prioritizing – Developing creativity
• Hands off – allow team to start the forming process	• Interpersonal skills – Personal styles/social style/people-are-different perceptions – Giving and receiving feedback – Dialogue skills (in the Senge sense)
• Assume referee-type role in storming process	• Interpersonal skills: – Confrontation – Conflict resolution – Negotiating skills (win/win brand)
• Hands off again as norming starts to develop	• Woo woo – perhaps the great outdoors: – Raising personal awareness – Personal empowerment – Breakthrough/changing the game
• Bring the woo woo back to the business sessions as the performing stage emerges	

Choosing the right external partners for training is really very important. Trainers are an integral part of the change process being implemented and so they must:

- be compatible with the organization's staff – acceptable kinds of people;
- be briefed at the mission, vision and values level so that they clearly reinforce the consistency of these critical underlying strata;
- actively support each individual team's objectives, measurement criteria, feedback loops etc.;
- be around for the duration – i.e. same trainers throughout;
- be capable of consistency across the organization – each team's experience of external trainers must be the same.

It also helps if a training organization either has its own psycho-metric tools, or access to, and competence with, the tools of other organizations. Such psychometric tools may not serve a usable predictive purpose but they help to raise awareness of team processes. For example, as suggested earlier, Belbin's team roles may not be a viable basis on which to form teams, but they provide an excellent basis on which to predicate a dialogue about what should be going on inside the team.

Other training organizations have team profile instruments. These differ from instruments such as Belbin Team Roles in that they often measure the climate in the team, issues of trust, degree of alignment, interpersonal friction and so on. This can help diagnose problems and set up performance improvement. All of these instruments need some form of evaluation to determine their fit with the organization's style, systems and priorities.

Some training companies have developed programmes and tools which facilitate and speed up the way in which the team reaches agreement, for example around objectives, priorities, critical success factors etc. A few of these are computer driven and provide instantaneous feedback to the group. These are particularly effective.

Subsume all the stakeholders

Often an organization's focus is so resolutely fixed upon the teams that are being developed that others parts of the organization are overlooked.

We have spoken at length about the change of roles of middle managers and supervisors as a result of developing teaming. We know that the changes in function they go

156

through are almost always unexpected and sometimes unsatisfactory. It goes without saying that the intelligent organization provides the retraining and development of these people as well.

If parts of the organization fall outside the teaming activity, and this is often the case, these segments must be looked after too. Context and organizational intent must be shared, information must be provided, updates discussed, briefing provided etc.

It is probably true to say that most organizations underestimate the amount of internal publicity and briefing which must be provided, and also the range of people to whom it must be provided. Sometimes it makes sense to develop new internal media to help cement the idea and contribution of teaming into the organization. Think in terms of over-providing information and briefing, and you will still fall short.

Among the things that have contributed to successful implementation is developing new recognition systems within the organization. These need not be expensive compensation systems, although an element of reward assists them. The Toyota case (Chapter 6) outlines some clever applications. It takes some thinking about and a little ingenuity; it need not cost much.

Allies

It really helps the manager confronting a programme of team development if (s)he can find well-placed allies within the organization. These should, if possible, be people situated higher up the tree who are prepared to support the team in organizational forums to which you as manager may not have access. Americans refer to this as 'riding shot-gun' for the team. This stems, I think, from the armed man (I think they were only ever men) who rode in a visible position on the stagecoach. His visibility discouraged stick-ups and hijacks, but if they occurred he blazed away at the villains.

The value of the organizational equivalent is not hard to imagine, though (s)he might be hard to find. In any event, be under no illusion, this is a valuable piece of assistance to be able to access.

As with any significant organizational change, the quality of the planning for implementation, and the anticipation shown before activity commences, usually determine the degree of success of the initiative. This is no less true of teaming, but in that the resulting organization is likely to be radically different from the way it was, perhaps even more imaginative foresight is needed.

Planning questionnaire

1. What are the consequences of starting out and failing? Three answers please:
    - Personal consequences?
    - Consequences for those who were involved in the failed attempt?
    - Broader organizational consequences?

2. What (besides the Ten Steps) will I have to do to succeed?
    - How do I stop the organization killing it off?
    - Do I know in what respects my role will change as a result?
    - Can I/Do I want to change what I do to the degree that will be necessary for the team to succeed?

3. Can I access the resources?
    - Hard costs: IT, work stations etc.?
    - Soft-side costs and suppliers: training, consultants, meetings?
    - Opportunity cost; can I assess, can I minimize?

4. What are the consequences of succeeding? Four answers please:
    - Personal consequences?
    - Consequences for those who are now a high performing team?
    - Broader organizational consequences?
    - Will we be able to use high performing teams long term; will the organization meet their needs, will they meet the the organizations needs?

5. Is this the best time to try it? Might there be a better . . . a worse . . .?

Other important things to think about

6. Who will I have to get on board inside the organization to support this? Try to compile a detailed strategy which might look like:

Person's name	Positives for that person (to stress)	Negatives for that person (to minimize)

7. Who are the best training people to use?
    How do I qualify them/test them/get the best out of them?

8. Are there other external resources I might need? Consultants?

9. Internal roll-out and public relations: try to compile a programme with as much seriousness as you would if launching a new product to an uncaring market.

10. Reward/recognition systems I might be able to use:
    ... in the team   ... outside it

11. Allies I might enlist (people to ride shot-gun); how to get them on board?

12. All the things I have not thought about above ...

14 Where to find out more

This chapter gives a very biased and personal account of the best sources of more information. It does not attempt to be comprehensive, rather it is selective.

The best books

There are a number of titles published on both sides of the Atlantic which cover teams and empowerment. The following list is a personal selection – you could read much more broadly, but I doubt that you would find anything to add substantially to the formidable range of wisdom and experience represented below.

Belbin: Management Teams. Why they Succeed or Fail
    Butterworth-Heinemann, 1983
    An oldie but goody. Belbin writes extremely well and tells an interesting story about seminal development of research into teaming. Provides excellent context.
Belbin: Team Roles at Work
    Butterworth-Heinemann, 1993
    A more recent update of Belbin's thinking with the added richness of a number of years of additional research and development – an intriguing read.
Katzenbach and Smith: The Wisdom of Teams: Creating the High Performance Organization
    Harvard Business School Press, 1993
    A thoughtful and informed book drawing on the experience of McKinsey. A worthwhile read though you have to overlook the inevitable McKinsey hauteur.

Where to find out more

Robbins and Finley: Why Teams Don't Work. What Went Wrong and How to Make it Right
Peterson's Pacesetter Books, 1995
Fast-paced, irreverently written but essentially well-informed book – good to dip in and out of. One of the Financial Times books of the year 1995.

Senge: The Fifth Discipline. The Art and Practice of the Learning Organization
Doubleday, 1990
Only tangentially about teaming but a formidably wise book which points the way to the organizational values of the future.

Wellins, Byham and Wilson: Empowered Teams. Creating Self Directed Work Groups that Improve Quality, Productivity and Participation
Jossey-Bass, 1991
Just as the title tries to leave nothing out, so the book aims to be, and pretty well succeeds in being, comprehensive. At its heart is a now rather out-of-date survey of teaming undertaken by DDI, but the lessons and the experience of the company remain valid.

Note: following this section there is also a complete bibliography of other sources used in the writing of the book.

Journals

All the management journals, most personnel publications, training and development journals and journals about quality carry articles, case reports and studies on teams and team building.

An automated literature search of recent articles on teams and teaming surfaces:

Team Performance Management – MCB University Press, Quarterly

as the most frequently recurring source. This is a fairly uncritical recommendation.

Literature search

More valuable to the manager looking for help is to gain access to literature search and information services, who will perform keyword searches of databases and produce reading and citation lists. I recommend two:

(1) The **Institute of Management Foundation**: Phone +44 (0)1536 204222; Fax +44 (0)1536 401013.

You can subscribe to the IM service and experience a level of service, support and added value which is exceptional. IM will supply you with:

- reprints of journal articles from their extensive collection;
- reprints, at additional cost, of journal articles not in their collection;
- a book loan service.

(2) I have also used, with success, a service on the Internet called **IQUEST** which I have accessed through CompuServe. IQUEST presents a number of databases (including the Harvard Business Review) which allow fast and efficient, low-cost keyword searches.

This will identify interesting-sounding journal articles. Another level of interrogation (and cost) will provide summaries and a reprint ordering service also exists.

Of course, if you have access to a university or good college library, similar services may be available to you.

Training companies

162

As I have indicated elsewhere, the range of training companies and individual consultants offering team building is almost limitless. Those I have listed reflect, of course, a very personal bias of experience and association. While I do think it is important to acknowledge this, I do not apologize for it.

Where to find out more

To be comprehensive is the province of directories and databases; to be selective provides the reader with the gift of experience.

Three organizations providing good consultancy, practical hands-on training, an international scope of operations and a wide generic base of material which can be tailored are:

- Wilson Learning,
  7500 Flying Cloud Drive
  Eden Prairie
  MN55344 3795 USA
  Phone +(1) 612 944 2880
  Fax   +(1) 612 828 8835

  Wilson Learning (GB)
  23 London End,
  Beaconsfield,
  Bucks. HP9 2HN UK
  + (44) (0)1494 678121
  + (44) (0)1494 678631

One of the things which distinguishes Wilson is what it calls its INNOVATOR technology. This is one of the most effective team development processes I know, providing interactive computer-based polling systems which allow teams to reach rapid consensus on objectives, priorities, differences and other team issues.

- Development Dimensions
  International
  1225 Washington Pike
  Bridgeville
  PA 15017 2838 USA
  Phone +(1) 412 257 0600
  Fax   +(1) 412 257 3093

  DDI (UK) Ltd
  Keystone House
  Loudwater
  Bucks HP10 9PY UK

  +(44) (0)1628 810800
  +(44) (0)1628 810320

DDI's principals are the authors of Empowered Teams, a book recommended above.

- Zenger Miller
  1735 Technology Drive
  San Jose
  CA 95110 1313 USA
  Phone +(1) 408 452 1244
  Fax   +(1) 408 452 1155

  TMT Europe
  250 Gunnersby Avenue
  London W4 5QB UK

  +(44) (0)181 994 8592
  +(44) (0)181 747 1398

Zenger Miller has become part of the mighty Times Mirror Training organization. TMT offers a broad range of training, development and consultancy through a number of associated companies which it owns.

High Performing Teams

Two addresses are given above, but for all three organizations, international headquarters are in the USA. Each has offices around the world and can operate in several languages.

They are also mentioned in Chapter 3, 'How the High Performing Team Concept Developed'.

Two specialist UK organizations worth mentioning are:

- Saville & Holdsworth
  3 AC Court
  High Street
  Thames Ditton
  Surrey KT7 OSR
  Phone +(44) (0)181 398 4170
  Fax   +(44) (0)181 398 9544

Saville & Holdsworth are occupational psychologists and have a broad and impressive base of psychometric tools (which cover for example Belbin's roles). Use of appropriate configurations of these tools can, as we have discussed elsewhere, enhance a team's understanding of its own interactions.

- The Europe Japan Centre
  Nash House
  St George Street
  London W1R 9DE
  Phone +(44) (0) 171 491 1791
  Fax   +(44) (0) 171 491 4055

Europe Japan Centre specializes in training and development associated with Kaizen – continuous improvement – which is especially associated with quality circle approaches. It is owned by Osaka Gas and is an interesting bridge across which Japanese management thinking is transferred to Europe.

Some direct access

- **Michael Colenso** – E-mail: 101733,2337@compuserve.com.

  Always interested in teaming applications, case studies, experiences or hang-ups.

- **Harvey Robbins** – E-mail: robbi004@maroon.tc.umn.edu

  'would like to hear your team experiences – what problems you ran into, what solutions you came up with'

  Robbins is co-author of Why Teams Don't Work – see above.

Bibliography and reference

The first digit below indicates the number of the chapter in which the work is first cited.

2.1   Robbins and Finley: Why Teams Don't Work. What Went Wrong and How to Make it Right
Peterson's/Pacesetter Books, 1995

2.2   Wetlaufer: The Team That Wasn't
Harvard Business Review, Nov–Dec 1994

2.3   Tomorrow's Company: The Role Of Business in a Changing World
The Royal Society for the ecouragements of Arts, Manufactures and Commerce, 1995

3.1   Belbin: Management Teams. Why they Succeed or Fail
Heinemann, 1981

3.2   Belbin: Team Roles at Work
Butterworth-Heinemann, 1993

3.3   Harvey-Jones: Making it Happen. Reflections on Leadership
Collins, 1988

3.4   Zenger, Musselwhite, Hurson and Perrin: Leading Teams: Mastering the New Role
Irwin, 1993

3.5   Wellins, Byham and Wilson: Empowered Teams. Creating Self Directed Work Groups that Improve Quality, Productivity and Participation
Jossey-Bass, 1991

...in brief

Bibliography and reference

3.6   Senge: The Fifth Discipline: The Art and Practice of
       The Learning Organization
       Doubleday, 1990

4.1   Peters and Waterman: In Search of Excellence
       Harper & Row, 1984

4.2   Heller: The Fate of IBM
       Warner Books, 1994

5.1   Temple and Droege: Internal Customers Need
       Delighting Too. Managing Service Quality, Vol. 4
       No. 1 1994, MCB Press

5.2   Rea: The Role of Teams in a New Company
       Team Performance Management Journal, Vol. 1
       No. 1 1995 MCB Press

5.3   Semler: Maverick!
       Random House, 1993

6.1   Feature Article: Key Issues in Effective Teamworking
       Employee Development Bulletin 69, September 1995

6.2   Scott: The Apparatus Business in BT – A Team Story
       Team Performance Management Journal, Vol. 1
       No. 3, 1995 MCB Press

6.3   Ranney and Deck: Making Teams Work: Lessons
       from the Leaders in New Product Development
       Planning Review, July–Aug 1995

6.4   Besser: Rewards and Organizational Goal
       Achievement: A Case Study of Toyota Motor
       Manufacturing in Kentucky
       Journal of Management Studies, 323, May 1995

6.5   Yeatts, Hipskind and Barnes: Lessons Learned from
       Self Managed Work Teams
       Business Horizons, July–Aug 1994

6.6   Newton: Expressing Commitment
       Best Practice UK, May 1995

6.7   Arthur: Rover Managers Learn to Take a Back Seat
       Personnel Management, October 1994

6.8   Rowland: Come and Be Taken Seriously
       Team Performance Management Journal, Vol. 1
       No. 1, 1995 MCB Press

6.9 Katzenbach and Smith: The Wisdom of Teams: Creating the High Performance Organization
Harvard Business School Press, 1993

6.10 Amason: Distinguishing the Effects of Functional and Dysfunctional Conflict on Strategic Decision Making: Resolving a Paradox for Top Management Teams
Academy of Management Journal, Vol 39, No. 1, February 1986

6.11 Bowman and Carter: Organising for Competitive Advantage
European Management Journal, Vol. 13 No. 4, Elsevier

6.12 Kennedy: Managing Without Managers
Director, October 1994

6.13 Johnson: Industrial Dispute in Royal Mail. The CWU Position
Communication Workers Union, 1995

7.1 Drummond: The Quality Movement
Kogan Page, 1992

8.1 Ainsworth-Land: Grow or Die
Reissued Edition, John Wiley, 1986

8.2 Owen: Creating Top Flight Teams
Kogan Page, 1996

10.1 Hammer and Stanton The Reengineering Revolution Handbook
Harper Collins,1996

10.2 Handy: Inside Organisations
BBC Books, 1990

10.3 The Leader Manager
A Wilson Learning Management Training Programme

11.1 Porter: Competitive Strategy
Free Press, 1980

11.2 D'Aveni: Hypercompetition. Where Traditional Strategies Can be a Deadly Distraction
Wilson Learning, 1994

Bibliography and reference

11.3 Pedlar, Burgoyne and Boydell: Towards The Learning Company: Concepts and Practices
McGraw-Hill, 1991

11.4 Hickman and Silva: The Future 500. Creating Tomorrow's Organisations Today
Unwin Hyman, 1987

Index

Index

6239 70